John Warton

Poems

Original and Translated

John Warton

Poems
Original and Translated

ISBN/EAN: 9783744712095

Printed in Europe, USA, Canada, Australia, Japan

Cover: Foto ©Thomas Meinert / pixelio.de

More available books at **www.hansebooks.com**

ORIGINAL AND TRANSLATED,

BY THE

REV. JOHN WARTON, M.A.

CONTENTS.

	PAGE
THE Complaint	1
The Pyramids of Egypt	10
Rex Fluviorum Thamesis	14
Part of the First Book of the Argonautics of Apollonius Rhodius	19
Solitude at an Inn	59
Epitaph	61
To a Painter	62
From the Greek of Simonides	63
From the Greek of Apollonius Rhodius	65
A Sacred Anacreontic Ode	68
The Vision of Moses	71
In Horto Script. Auctore T. Warton	77
The foregoing imitated	78
Polydore and Cleonice, a Tale in Imitation of Dryden	80
Alfredus	101

CONTENTS.

	Page
Antipatri ex Anthologia	109
Incerti Auctoris ex Anthologia	110
Callimachi ex Anthologia	111
Inscriptio	112
Uxori Opt.	113
Elegia	114
Archiæ ex Anthologia	116
Parmenionis ex Anthologia	117
Dioscoridis ex Anthologia	118
Antipatri ex Anthologia	119
Inscribed on a Beautiful Grotto near the Water	120
Idem Latinè Redditum	121
Ex Anthologia	122
An Ars sit Perfectior Natura? Affirmatur	123
An Locus Conveniat Locato? Affirmatur	124
An Casus et Fortuna sint in Rebus? Affirmatur	126
Incerti Auctoris ex Anthologia	128
——Dulcique Animos Novitate Tenebat	129
In Sylva Script.	130
Pictori Egregio Thomæ Beach	131
Epitaphium Annæ Staines	133

SUBSCRIBERS.

A.

ABRAHAM, Mr.
Adams, Rev. James, fellow of New college, Oxford, *four copies*
Addington, Rt. Hon. H. fpeaker of the H. of Commons, *four copies*
Addington, J. H. Efq. Blount's-Court, Henly, *four copies*
Alexander, ———, Efq. alderman of Dublin
Alexander, Rev. J. W. fellow of Trinity college, Oxford
Alcock, Rev. Charles, Hindon, Suffex
Allen, Mr. Jefferys
Allen, Mr. George
Allen, Mr.
Ambrofe, Rev. John, Poulton, Gloucefterfhire
Ambrofe, Mrs. Poulton, Gloucefterfhire
Anftey, John, Efq. Lincoln's-Inn
Armftrong, Mr. J.
Afhe, Rev. Robert, Southampton, *two copies*
Afhe, Mrs. *two copies*
Afhurft, Lady
Atherley, A. Efq. Southampton
Atkins, Samuel, Efq. Wickham, Hants
Auften, Richard, Efq. Wimborne, Dorfet
Auften, Rev. J. Enfbury, Hants
Awbrey, Rev. John, fellow of New college, Oxford, *four copies*

B.

Baker, Mrs. Canterbury, *two copies*
Baker, Rev. Dr. Sarum
Ball, Rev. John, Winfrith, Dorſet
Baldock, Rev. C. B. Milton-Abbas, Dorſet
Ballard, Robert, Eſq. Southampton
Bampfylde, Rev. Richard
Banniſter, Rev. Mr.
Barnes, Rev. Mr. Chicheſter
Barnes, John, Eſq.
Bargus, Rev. Thomas
Barne, Snowden, Eſq. Inner-Temple
Barkley, William, Eſq. Middle-Temple, *two copies*
Barkley, capt. John, Lord Hawkeſbury Indiaman, *two copies*
Barwell, Richard, Eſq. *four copies*
Barwell, Mrs. *four copies*
Bartholemew, Rev. Robert, head maſter of Exeter ſchool
Bartlet, Thomas, Eſq. Wareham
Baſkett, Rev. Richard
Baſket, Rev. John, Blandford St. Mary
Baſkett, Rev. Kingſman, Trinity college, Cambridge
Baſtard, Mrs. John, Blandford, Dorſet
Bathurſt, Rev. Charles, New college, Oxford, *two copies*
Baxter, Alexander, Eſq.
Baynes, Rev. John, Droxford, Hants
Baynes, Mr. T.
Beach, Mr. T. Kew
Beach, Miſs, Kew
Beardmore, Rev. Dr. warden of Merton college, Oxford, *two copies*
Beaufort, His Grace the Duke of
Belin, Mr. Wincheſter, *two copies*
Bellamont, the Right Hon. Earl of, K. B.
Bellamy, Rev. Andrew, Chetnole, Dorſet

[iii]

Bellamy, Mr. Exeter college, Oxford
Benet, Rev. John, LL. D. Donhead, Wilts
Benfley, William, Efq. *two copies*
Benwell, Rev. Mr. fellow of Trinity college, Oxford
Berresford, Right Hon. John
Bertie, colonel
Biggs, Mr. Robert, Blandford
Bingham, Richard, Efq. Bingham's-Melcombe, Dorfet
Bingham, Rev. George, Pimperne, Dorfet, *four copies*
Bingham, Mifs, Pimperne, Dorfet
Bingham, Rev. Peregrine, Ratcliffe, Bucks, *two copies*
Blackftone, Rev. Charles, fen. fellow of Winton college
Blackftone, Rev. Charles, jun. fellow of Winton college
Blackftone, James, Efq. Inner-Temple
Blackftone, ———, Efq. New college, Oxford
Blair, Rev. William, New college, Oxford
Blaquiere, Right Hon. Sir John, K. B.
Blaquiere, Lady
Blunt, Mrs. Lower-Wallop, Hants
Blount, G. L. Efq. Southampton
Blount, Rev. Mr. *two copies*
Blunt, S. Efq.
Bluet, ———, Efq. *four copies*
Bolingbroke, Lady, *four copies*
Bond, John, Efq. M. P.
Bond, Nathaniel, Efq. Inner-Temple
Bond, Mifs
Bond, Rev. Thomas
Bond, Rev. William
Boor, Mr. Southampton
Bofanquet, Henry, Efq. Langford-Court, Somerfet
Bouverie, Hon. William Henry
Bouverie, Hon. B.
Bouverie, Hon. Edward

Bowdler, Mrs.
Bowdler, Miſs Harriet
Bowles, Rev. Mr. Sarum
Bowles, Rev. W. L. Donhead
Bowles, Henry, M. D. Winton
Bowles, Mr. Charles, Shaſton
Boyer, Edward, Eſq. *two copies*
Boyle, Lady Jane, Hazle-Grove, near Sherborne
Boynton, Sir Griffith, Bart.
Boynton, Lady
Bradford, Mr.
Bramſtone, Mr. New college, Oxford
Bracher, John Kellow. Eſq. Trinity college, Oxford
Brereton, Rev. J. Alton-Barnes
Brine, James, Eſq. Blandford
Brice, Rev. G. Wareham
Bricknell, Rev. Mr.
Briſcoe, Rev. Mr. Aſhton-Keynes
Briſted, Rev. N. Biſhop's-Caundle, Dorſet
Briſtow, W. Eſq.
Broderip, Mr. Briſtol, *two copies*
Bromfield, capt. Lymington
Bromfield, Mr. Lymington
Brooch, Rev. Cudworth, Univerſity college, Oxford
Broughton, Lady, Red-Rice, near Andover
Brown, Mrs. Eaſt-Street, Queen's-Square, London
Brown, Barwell, Eſq. *two copies*
Browning, Rev. Dr. Frederick
Browning, Mrs.
Brudenell, Mrs.
Bruhl, Miſs.
Bryant, Jacob, Eſq.
Buckner, Rev. Dr. *two copies*
Burch, Mr. S.

Burdon, Rev. George, Farnham, Surry
Burdon, Mr. Winchester, *twelve copies*
Burgess, Rev. Thomas, D. D. *two copies*
Burke, Richard, Esq. Lincoln's-Inn
Burlton, William, Esq. *four copies*
Burmingham, Mr. H.
Burmingham, Mr. T.
Burrard, Rev. G. Merton college, Oxford
Burrough, Rev. John Willis, Blandford St. Mary
Burrough, Rev. Thomas, Abbot's-Anne, Hants
Burrough, James, Esq. Hall-Stair-Case, Inner-Temple
Burrough, Miss
Burrough, Miss, Laverstock, Wilts
Burrough, Mrs. Sarum
Busby, Rev. William, New college, Oxford, *four copies*
Butson, Edward, D. D. dean of Waterford, Ireland
Butt, Rev. Edward, Wimborne
Butler, Rev. Thomas, Okeford, Fitzpaine
Butler, Rev. William, Sturminster-Newton

C.

Cabanal, ———, Esq.
Calcraft, John, Esq. Rempstone, Purbeck
Carhampton, Right Hon. Earl of
Carr, Rev. Mr. *two copies*
Cashell, His Grace the Arch-bishop of
Castleman, William, Esq. Wimborne
Cator, Joseph, Esq. Beckenham, Kent
Cavan, Right Hon. Dowager, Countess of
Cavan, Right Hon. Earl of, Sackville-Street
Cavan, Right Hon. Countess of
Chawte, Mr. Winchester
Chafy, Rev. John, Somerton

Chambers, Mr.
Chamberlayne, William, Esq. fellow of New college, Ox. *four copies*
Champion, Mrs. *two copies*
Chapman, Thomas, Esq. Inner-Temple
Chedworth, Right Hon. Lord, Ipswich
Chelsum, Rev. Dr. Droxford, Hants, *four copies*
Chesson, ———, Esq. New college, Oxford
Chichester, Mrs.
Chisholm, ———, Esq. Pembroke college, Oxford
Chudleigh, Miss, Chalmington, Dorset
Clarke, Rev. G. S. fellow of Trinity college, Oxford, *two copies*
Cleeves, Rev. John, Ringwood
Clonmell, Right Hon. Visc. chief justice of King's Bench, Ireland
Clunie, col. Macpherson, 3d guards, Downing-Street, *two copies*
Coker, John, Esq. Inner-Temple
Collins, Rev. Mr. *four copies*
Collings, Leo. Esq. *two copies*
Collins, James, Esq.
Colson, Rev. John, Studland
Compton, John, Esq. *four copies*
Conquest, Mr. Birmingham
Constable, William Maxwell, Esq.
Cooke, Rev. Mr. Bristol
Cooper, Rev. Dr.
Cooper, Mrs.
Cooth, Edmund, Esq. Blandford
Cooth, Rev. Samuel
Cotton, Joseph, Esq. London assurance, *two copies*
Cotton, John, Esq. Gower-Street, Bedford-Square, *two copies*
Cowper, Charles, Esq. Middle-Temple
Cox, William, Esq. Lincoln's-Inn-Fields
Coxe, Rev. William, Bemerton, Wilts, *two copies*
Cromleholme, Rev. Mr.
Cromleholme, Mrs.

Crofs, Mr.
Croffe, Rev. Robert, Blandford
Crowther, Mr. New college, Oxford
Cruttwell, Mr. Bath
Cumming, Rev. John Penrofe, New college, Oxford
Cunyngham, Right Hon. William, Dublin
Cure, George, Efq.
Cutler, Rev. Mr. head mafter of the grammar fchool, Sherborne

D.

Dacres, Mrs. Southampton
Dally, ———, Bridport
Dallas, Robert, Efq, Lincoln's-Inn
Dalton, Nathaniel, Efq. Shank's-Houfe, Dorfet
Dalton, John, Efq. Pitcombe, Somerfet
Dalton, Mifs, Shank's-Houfe
Dalton, Henry, Efq. *two copies*
Dampier, Henry, Efq. Middle-Temple
Dampier, Rev. J. Codford, Wilts
Dampier, Rev. Dr. dean of Rochefter
Dampier, Rev. Mr. Weftmeon, Hants
Danfey, Mr. William, Blandford
Danfey, Mr. J. Blandford
D'Auvergne, major-general, Southampton
D'Auvergne, col. Chatham
Davies, Devereux, Efq. Exchequer-Houfe, *two copies*
Davies, Rev. John, fellow of Trinity college, Oxford
Davis, Rev. Dr. provoft of Eton college
Dawfon, Mifs
Day, Mrs.
De la Pole, Sir John, Shute-Houfe, Devon, *four copies*
Dean, William, Efq. Wimborne, Dorfet
Debrifay, Jafper, Efq. Dublin

Deverell, Mr. Winchester
Dickenson, Charles, Esq.
Dobson, M. D. Sarum
Dodwell, Rev. A. Sarum
Douglas, Daniel, Esq.
Down, capt. James, Montrose Indiaman, *two copies*
Dowland, Rev. James, Whitchurch, Dorset
Downe, Mr. N. Bridport
Drewe, ———, jun. Esq. Chichester
Dring, Jeremiah, Esq.
Drinkwater, Mr.
Dundas, capt. James, Earl Fitzwilliam Indiaman, *two copies*
Dundas, capt. Ralph, Prince William Henry Indiaman, *two copies*
Durnford, T. Esq. Poole
Durnford, Charles, Esq. Boswell-Court
Dutton, Mr. Birmingham

E.

Eagland, Mr. John Sharp, St. Edmund's hall, Oxford
Eames, ———, Esq.
Earle, William Benson, Esq. Sarum
East, Edward Hyde, Esq. Lincoln's-Inn
Easton, Mr. E. Sarum
Eaton, Rev. John, Fairstead, Essex
Edwards, J. P. Esq. University college, Oxford
Egremont, Right Hon. Countess of
Ekins, Rev. Mr. New college, Oxford
Elliot, Hon. John, M. P. Bedford-Square
Ellis, Rev. Mr.
Ellis, Mrs. Hatton-Street, London
Elphinstone, Right Hon. Lord, Grafton-Street, *two copies*
Elphinstone, Right Hon. Lady, Grafton-Street, *two copies*
Elphinstone, Hon. Miss M.

Elphinstone, Hon. Miss C.
Elphinstone, Hon. Mrs. Mortimer-Street, Cav.-Square, *two copies*
Elphinstone, Hon. G. Keith, Grafton-Street, *two copies*
England, Rev. Mr. Stafford, Dorset.
Erle, Rev. Christopher, Fifehide-Mag. Dorset
Estcourt, Rev. Dr.
Ewer, Walter, Esq. *two copies*
Exeter, Right Hon. Earl of, *two copies*
Eyres, Mrs.
Eyres, George, Esq. jun.

F.

Fairfull, capt. Robert, Minerva Indiaman, *two copies*
Fairside, ——, Esq.
Falmouth, Right Hon. Visc. *four copies*
Farquharson, James, Esq. Littleton, Dorset, *twelve copies*
Farquharson, capt. James, Alfred Indiaman, *two copies*
Farquharson, Mrs. Harley-Street, *two copies*
Fazakerly, John, Esq. Sarum
Ferrers, Rev. Mr. *four copies*
Ffolliott, John, Esq. Trinity college, Oxford
Filkes, Rev. J. Trinity college, Oxford
Fitch, Henry William, Esq. High-Hall, Dorset
Fitzherbert, Miss, Blandford, Dorset
Fitzgibbon, Right Hon. John, Baron, Lord Chancellor of Ireland
Fitzhugh, V. Esq. *two copies*
Fitzhugh, ——, Esq.
Fitzhugh, William, Esq. *four copies*
Flamank, Rev. Dr. fellow of Trinity college, Oxford, *two copies*
Fletcher, Rev. N.
Foster, Rev. Thomas
Fox, Hon. Miss
Foxcroft, Rev. Mr. Stapleton

Foyle, Mr. sen.
Foyle, Mr. jun.
Franklin, Samuel, Esq. Inner-Temple
Fraser, Thomas, Esq. *two copies*
Fraser, Simon, Esq. of Lovat, Inner-Temple, *two copies*
Fraser, Simon, Esq. Coleman-Street, *two copies*
Fraser, Simon, Esq. jun. Coleman-Street, *two copies*
Fraser, James, Esq. Golden-Square, *two copies*
Fraser, Mrs. ditto, *two copies*
Fraser, William, Esq. Queen's-Square, *two copies*
Fraser, Mrs. ditto, *two copies*
Fraser, capt. J. of Invalids, *two copies*
Fraser, Mr. George, N° 9, 'Change-Alley
Fraser, Hugh, Esq. *two copies*
Fraser, Alexander, Esq. Staple's-Inn, *two copies*
Fullarton, col. *five copies*
Fuller, William, Esq. Sarum, *two copies*
Fyler, ——, Esq. Southampton

G.

Gale, Rev. John, Combe-Flory, Somerset, *ten copies*
Gape, John, Esq. Bath
Gardiner, Sir John Whalley Smythe, Bart. *two copies*
Garnier, George, Esq. Wickham, Hants, *two copies*
Garnier, Mrs. *two copies*
Garnier, capt. *two copies*
Garnier, lieut. Charles, *two copies*
Garnier, Mr. New college, Oxford
Gartshore, Maxwell, M. D. F. R. S. F. A. S.
Gauntlett, Carew, Esq. Winchester
Gauntlett, Peter, Esq. Winchester
Gauntlett, Rev. Mr. Hansley
Gawler, Henry, Esq. Lincoln's-Inn

Gayton, Rev. George Clark
Geary, Rev. Mr. fellow of Trinity college, Oxford, *two copies*
Gibbs, Vicary, Efq. Middle-Temple
Gibbs, Rev. Mr. Amefbury
Gladwell, Richard, Efq. Dublin
Glyn, Sir ——, Knt. *two copies*
Goddard, Ambrofe, Efq. M. P. *four copies*
Goddard, Rev. Mr. head mafter of Winchefter fchool, *two copies*
Good, Rev. Henry, Wimborne, Dorfet
Goodden, Wyndham, Efq. Middle-Temple
Goodden, Robert, Efq. Compton-Houfe, Dorfet
Goodden, Rev. John, Compton, Dorfet
Golding, Mr. Henry
Gore, T. Efq.
Gore, Mrs.
Gould, Sir Henry, Lincoln's-Inn-Square
Gould, Lady
Goulding, William, Efq.
Goulding, Mr.
Græme, Charles, Efq. *two copies*
Gray, Mr.
Gray, Mrs. North-Parade, Bath
Grand, G. F. Efq. *two copies*
Gregorie, Mrs. Berner's-Street, *two copies*
Grieve, Mr.
Griffith, Edmund, Efq. Briftol
Griffith, Mr. Merton college, Oxford
Grove, Rev. Thomas, Orchefton
Grove, Thomas, Efq. Ferne, Dorfet, *four copies*
Grofvenor, Richard, Erle-Drax, *two copies*
Grubb, Rev. Mr. Sarum
Guitton, Mrs. Wickham, Hants
Guitton, Mifs, Wickham, Hants
Guitton, Mifs, Wickham, Hants

Gundry, T. Esq. Dewlish, Dorset
Gunthorpe, William, Esq. Southampton, *four copies*
Guy, Rev. Mr. Chichester

H.

Hall, Rev. Henry, Child-Okeford, Dorset
Halton, Rev. L. G. Southampton
Hamilton, Sir Alexander, Retreat, Exeter, *two copies*
Hamilton, Lady, Retreat, Exeter, *two copies*
Hanham, Rev. James, Corfe-Mullen, Dorset
Harben, Wyndham, Esq. *four copies*
Hardy, Miss, Bridport
Harrison, Samuel, Esq. *two copies*
Hartley, Mrs. M.
Hartley, ——, Esq. Merton college, Oxford, *two copies*
Harvest, Rev. Mr. at Mr. Skelton's, Southampton, *two copies*
Harvey, John, Esq. Francis-Street, Bedford-Square, *two copies*
Harris, Rev. Mr. Sturminster-Marshal, Dorset
Harris, Miss Louisa, Spring-Gardens, London
Haviland, Mr. New college, Oxford
Hay, John, Esq.
Hayes, Philip, music doctor, *two copies*
Hayes, Rev. John
Hayter, ——, Esq.
Hawes, Rev. Herbert, Oriel college, Oxford
Hawes, Rev. Mr. Fisherton-Anger
Hawes, Mrs. Sarum
Hawes, Miss, Sarum
Hawley, W. H. T. Esq. *four copies*
Haynes, Chudleigh, Esq. *two copies*
Haynes, Mr.
Haynes, A. G. Esq. Southampton
Hawkins, Lady, Bath

Hearon, Miſs
Heathcote, Lady, *two copies*
Heathcote, Rev. Gilbert, New college, Oxford
Heber, ———, Eſq. Brazen-Noſe college, Oxford
Henville, Rev. Philip
Hepworth, capt. Earl of Mansfield Indiaman, *two copies*
Hencle, Rev. Nathaniel, Cheſter, *two copies*
Heywood, colonel, Southampton
Hill, colonel J.
Hill, Miſs Mary
Hodges, Walter Parry, Eſq. *four copies*
Hole, W. Eſq. Exeter college, Oxford
Hollingſworth, ———, Eſq. St. John's college, Oxford
Home, Mrs.
Hooper, Rev. Mr. fellow of Univerſity college, Oxford
Horne, Mr.
Horne, Mrs.
Horncaſtle, capt. James, Princeſs Royal Indiaman, *two copies*
Houlton Mr. J. Truro, Cornwall, *two copies*
Howley, Rev. Mr. New college, Oxford
Huddesford, Rev. G. St. Andrew's, Holborn, *two copies*
Hudſon, capt. Thomas, Cornwallis Indiaman, *two copies*
Hume, Alexander, Eſq. Gerrard-Street, Soho, *two copies*
Hume, Rev. Mr.
Hume, Mrs.
Hume, Miſs E. London
Hunter, Andrew, Eſq. *four copies*
Hunter, David, Eſq. *two copies*
Huntingford, Rev. G. J. D. D. warden of Winton college, *two copies*
Hurſt, Mr.
Hutton, Mrs. Blandford St. Mary
Hutton, Mrs. Harpur-Street, Queen's-Square
Hutton, Rev. Mr. fellow of Magdalen college, Oxford
Hyde, Rev. Humphry

J.

Jackson, Mrs. N° 1, Child's-Court, Fleet-Street
Jackson, Mrs. Portland-Place, Bath
Jackson, Rev. Richard, D.D.
Jackson, Rev. Gilbert
Jackson, Mr.
Jacob, Rev. Mr. Sarum
Jarrett, John, Esq. Freemantle, Hants, *four copies*
Jefferies, Rev. Mr. fellow of Winchester college
Jekyll, Joseph, M.P. Inner-Temple
Iles, Stephen, Esq. Upper-Cerne, Dorset
Ingilby, Rev. Mr.
Ingilby, Mrs.
Johnson, Mr.
Johnson, M.D. Birmingham
Johnson, Rev. Charles
Iremonger, Mrs. Wherwell, Hants
Iremonger, Miss
Iremonger, Rev. Lacelles, Lower-Clatford

K.

Kent, Rev. Mr. Southampton
Kerrich, Rev. Mr. New college, Oxford
King, Rev. Roe, Witchampton, Dorset
King, Mr. J. Tregonwell, Blandford
Knapton, Miss, Lymington, Hants
Kneller, John, Esq. Donhead, Wilts
Kneller, Miss
Knowles, Rev. Arthur

L.

Lance, ———, Efq. Southampton
Lance, Mrs. Southampton
Lanſdown, Right Hon. Marquis of, *four copies*
Lawrence, Mr. ſerjeant, Inner-Temple
Lawrence, Dr. Doctors-Commons, *two copies*
Laurie, L'Abbe, Dorcheſter
Lear, Rev. Mr. Downton, Wilts
Lee, Launcelot, Eſq. New college, Oxford
Lee, Mrs. Bath
Lee, H. N. Eſq. Wickham, Hants
Lee, Mrs. ditto
Lee, Miſs
Lee, Rev. Henry, fellow of Wincheſter college
Lee, Rev. William, *four copies*
Leer, Mr. Southampton, *two copies*
Leer, William, Eſq. Wimbórne, Dorſet
Lemerchant, James, Eſq. Southampton
Lemeſurier, Rev. Thomas, New college, Oxford
Lens, John, Eſq. Lincolns-Inn
Lenox, Lady Louiſa
Leverſuch, captain
Lightburne, ———, Eſq. alderman of Dublin
Liſter, Miſs, York
Litchfield, H. Charles, Eſq. Inner-Temple
Lloyd, William, Eſq. Sarum, *two copies*
Lloyd, captain, *ſix copies*
Lockton, Rev. John, Clanville, Hants
Lockton, John, Eſq. Pembroke college, Oxford
Long, lieut. Thomas, *four copies*
Lowth, Rev. Mr. prebendary of Winton
Lowth, Rev. Robert, *four copies*
Lucas, Rev. Richard

Lucas, Mrs.
Lutterell, Francis Fownes, Esq. Powis-Place
Lutterell, ——, Hon. Temple
Lutterell, Hon. Mrs.
Lyon, John, Esq. Middle-Temple

M.

Mackarell, Mrs. Beverly, Yorkshire
M'Donald, major, *two copies*
Mahon, Mr. John, Dublin, *two copies*
Mahon, Mr. William, *two copies*
Maitland, John, Esq.
Malmesbury, Right Hon. Lord, *ten copies*
Maltby, Mrs. Fishmongers'-Hall
Mansfield, Right Hon. Earl of
Mant, Rev. Dr. Southampton
Mapleton, M. D. Odiham, Hants
Mapleton, Mrs. Odiham, Hants
Mapleton, Mr. Odiham, Hants
Mapleton, Mr. J.
Mapleton, Miss
Mapleton, Miss, M. A.
March, Thomas, Esq. *two copies*
Marsh, Rev. George, *two copies*
Maton, W. G. Esq. Sarum
Maud, Mrs.
Maurice, Rev. Robert, Blandford
Maxwell, Henry, Esq.
Maycock, Rev. Henry
Mayo, Rev. James, Wimborne
Mead, Rev. Mr. Magdalen college, Oxford
Meech, Rev. Giles, *two copies*
Meech, Miss, Dorchester

Middleton, Rev. Mr. Chichester
Middleton, ———, Esq. Town-Hill, Hants
Middleton, Mrs. Town-Hill, Hants
Middleton, H. Esq.
Michell, Rev. Mr.
Michell, Rev. Mr. fellow of Wadham college, Oxford
Michell, Christopher, Esq.
Mills, Mr. Trinity college, Oxford
Mills, William, Esq. *two copies*
Mills, James, Esq. *two copies*
Miller, Mrs.
Mildmay, Sir Henry St. John, Bart.
Mildmay, Lady St. John
Mildmay, Mrs.
Mildmay, Miss
Milloway, Mr.
Mitchell, H. H. Esq. Dublin
Mitton, ———, Esq. *two copies*
Montgomery, Rev. Mr. South-Street, Grosvenor-Square
Moody, Rev. William, Great-Bathampton
Moore, Rev. Mr. Chichester
Morgan, colonel James, Southampton, *twenty copies*
Morgan, Mrs. Southampton, *twenty copies*
Morris, John, Esq. M. Boswell-Court
Morrison, Rev. Mr. fellow of New college, Oxford
Moss, Rev. Mr. canon of Sarum
Moulding, Rev. J. B. fellow of Trinity college, Oxford
Munton, Mr. Southampton
Murray, David, Esq.
Murray, Right Hon. Lord Charles, New college, Oxford
Muston, Mr. W. surgeon, Blandford

N.

Napier, Edward Berkley, Esq. Pile-House, Somerset
Newbolt, Rev. Mr. Winchester, *two copies*
Newland, Bingham, Esq. *four copies*
Newnham, Mr. J.
Newnham, Mr. C.
Newhouse, T. P. Esq. New college, Oxford
Norman, Samuel, Esq. Taunton
Norton, Hon. Baron, *four copies*

O.

O'Brien, Right Hon. Sir Lucius
Odell, Mrs.
Odell, Miss
Odell, Mr.
Odell, Mr. C.
Oglander, Sir William, Bart. *two copies*
Oglander, Rev. Mr. fellow of Winchester college, *two copies*
Oglander, Rev. Dr. warden of New college, Oxford, *six copies*
Oglander, Mr. New college, Oxford
Ogle, Right Hon. George, Dublin
Oldsworth, Rev. Mr. Hannington, Wilts
Ormsly, James, Esq.
Ossory, Right Rev. Bishop of
Owen, Mr.

P.

Page, Francis, Esq. M. P. University college, Oxford
Palmer, Mr.
Parkin, Rev. Mr.
Parkin, Mrs.
Parnell, Right Hon. Sir John, chancellor of the Exchequer, Ireland

Parsons, William, music doctor, master of the King's band
Paton, Andrew, Esq. *two copies*
Pell, ———, Esq. Trinity college, Oxford
Pell, Mrs. Southampton
Penny, Rev. Dr.
Penrose, Rev. Mr. New college, Oxford
Perrot, Thomas, Esq. University college, Oxford
Peyton, Sir Yelverton, Bart. Southampton
Phelips, Rev. Charles, *four copies*
Phillips, Rev. J. fellow of Exeter college, Oxford
Pickard, Rev. George, Warmwell
Pickford, J. D. M. D. Wimborne, Dorset
Pickering, Rev. Mr. Wickham, Hants
Pickering, ———, Esq. *four copies*
Pickering, Rev. Mr. Birmingham
Pinkerton, Mr.
Pitt, Right Hon. general
Pitt, George Frederic, Esq. Southampton, *two copies*
Pleydell, E. M. Esq. Milborn St. Andrew's, Dorset
Pockin, colonel
Pole, Rev. E. *four copies*
Pollen, Rev. Mr.
Pollock, ———, Esq.
Pollock, S. Fishmongers'-Hall
Pollock, Mr. Charlton, N° 15, Philpot-Lane
Pollock, Mr. T. N° 15, Philpot-Lane
Pooley, Rev. H. *four copies*
Poore, Mrs. High-Hall, Dorset
Portal, William, Esq. Inner-Temple
Powell, Mrs. Sarum
Powlett, Rev. Charles
Price, Rev. John, Trinity college, Oxford
Price, Joseph, sen. Esq. *three copies*
Price, Joseph, jun. Esq. *three copies*

Price, Bartholomew, Esq. Gloucester-Place, Mary-le-bone-Road
Pryce, Mr.
Pulteney, Richard, M.D. F.R.S. Blandford, *two copies*
Pulteney, Mrs. Blandford, *two copies*
Purbeck, Miss, Walcot-Parade, Bath
Purkis, William, D.D.
Pusey, Hon. Philip
Pye, Henry James, Esq. Poet-Laureat
Pyne, Rev. A.
Pyne, ——, Esq. *two copies*
Pyne, Mrs. *two copies*
Pyott, Mr. William
Pyott, Miss
Pyott, Miss A.

R.

Rackett, Rev. Thomas, Shaftesbury, Dorset
Rackett, Mrs.
Rackster, Mr. Bristol
Ranelagh, Right Hon. Visc.
Rashleigh, Rev. Mr. Silverton, Devon
Ravenhill, Rev. Mr. Cattistock, Dorset
Rawbone, Rev. Mr. vice princ. St. Mary's hall, Oxford
Read, James, Esq. Lincoln's-Inn
Reeve, Edward, Esq.
Rennell, Rev. Mr. jun. prebendary of Winchester
Renward, Mr. W.
Reynardson, Samuel, Esq.
Rhodes, Rev. Mr.
Richards, William, Esq. Warmwell, Dorset
Richards, Mr. W. New college, Oxford
Richards, Rev. Mr. Winchester
Richards, Mrs.

Ridout, Mrs.
Richardfon, Rev. John, Stickland, Dorfet
Richman, Rev. Mr. mafter of the grammar fchool, Dorchefter
Ricketts, George, Efq. *two copies*
Ricketts, Mrs. G.
Rivers, William, Efq. New college, Oxford
Rivers, Mr. St. Mary's hall, Oxford
Robinfon, Hon. Mr. Privy-Garden, London
Robinfon, Hon. Mrs.
Roeback, Mrs. Harpur-Street, Queen's-Square, *two copies*
Rogers, Rev. J. Okeford, Dorfet
Rolleftone, S. Efq. Southampton
Rook, Rev. Mr. R. jun. Southampton
Rooke, Mr. ferjeant, Effex-Street, London
Rothery, Rev. William, Hafilbury, Dorfet
Rothery, Mrs.
Ryves, George, Efq.

S.

Sadleir, R. V. Efq. Southampton, *two copies*
Sainfbury, H. Efq. St. John's college, Oxford
St. Barbe, Mrs. Southampton, *two copies*
St. Barbe, Mifs
St. John, Rev. William
St. John, Mifs Mary
St. John, Mrs. E.
Salmon, Rev. Mr.
Salter, Rev. Edward
Saltoun, Right Hon. Lord Alexander, *two copies*
Sampfon, Rev. Mr.
Scholfield, Rev. Mr. Trinity college, Oxford
Scott, Rev. Dr. Itchen, Hants
Scott, John Fenton, Efq.

Scott, Mrs.
Scott, Mrs.
Scutt, Mr. fellow of New college, Oxford
Seaman, Mrs. N° 4, Upper-Gower-Street
Sealy, John, Efq. King's-Bench-Walk, *two copies*
Second, Mr. Bath
Second, Mrs. Bath
Second, Mifs, Bath
Serle, Mr. C. E. N° 15, Philpot-Lane
Seward, ——, Efq. N° 5, Little-Maddox-Street, *four copies*
Seymour, Mrs.
Seyward, Mifs, Litchfield
Shaftefbury, Right Hon. Earl of, *two copies*
Shakefpear, John, Efq. *two copies*
Shannon, Right Hon. Earl of, Knt. St. Pk.
Shebbere, Mr.
Shepherd, Francis, Efq.
Sherer, Mr. J. Southampton
Sherive, Rev. C. H. Bridport
Sherive, Mrs. Bridport
Shipley, Mrs. *two copies*
Shipley, Mifs C. L.
Shuckburgh, C. W. Efq. Sarum
Simmonds, Mifs, Blandford
Sinclair, Sir John, Bart. M. P.
Siffmore, Rev. Mr. New college, Oxford, *two copies*
Skinner, Rev. Dr. mafter of the grammar fchool, Clofe, Sarum
Slingfby, Charles, Efq.
Slingfby, Thomas, Efq.
Slingfby, Sir Thomas, Bart.
Slingfby, Lady
Sloane, Mrs. H. Southampton
Smith, Rev. Mr. R. Winton, *two copies*
Smith, Rev. Charles, Aldermanbury

Smith, Rev. Charles, New college, Oxford
Smith, Mr. Courtney
Smyth, Rev. Philip, New college, Oxford, *four copies*
Snow, George, Esq. Langton, Dorset, *four copies*
Somerset, Right Hon. Lord Charles
Sothely, William, Esq. Southampton
Sothely, Thomas, Esq. Southampton
South, T. Esq. *two copies*
Sparrow, Rev. Mr. Bath
Speaker, Right Hon. of the House of Commons of Ireland
Stackhouse, Mr.
Stafford, Mrs.
Steele, Mrs. Chichester
Stainton, P. Esq. *two copies*
Starkey, Rev. Mr. Tokenham
Stevens, Henry, Esq. Trinity college, Oxford
Stevens, Rev. T. Bradfield, Berks
Steele, Miss, Broughton
Stephenson, George, Esq.
Steevens, Miss, Wimborne, Dorset
Steward, Gabriel, Esq. Weymouth
Still, Robert, Esq. Sarum, *two copies*
Stozey, Robert, Esq. Bedford-Square, *two copies*
Strong, Rev. Mr. Trinity college, Oxford
Stuart, Mr. Birmingham
Sturges, Mr. Christ-Church college, Oxford
Sturt, Ashley, Esq.
Summers, Rev. Dr. Bath
Swanton, Rev. Mr. Worthy, near Winchester
Symmonds, Mr. Bristol

T.

Tahourdin, Mr. G. jun.
Talbot, ———, Esq. *four copies*

Tatterſal, Rev. John, Otterden-Place, Kent
Tattarſal, Rev. William Dechair, Wootton-Underedge, Glouc.
Tatum, Thomas, Eſq. Sarum
Taunton, Rev. Dr. Bath
Taunton, Mrs. Bath
Taylor, John, Eſq. *ſix copies*
Taylor, Rev. E. fellow of Trinity college, Oxford, *two copies*
Templeman, Giles, Eſq. Middle-Temple
Templeman, Rev. N. Guſſage St. Michael's, Dorſet
Templeman, Mrs.
Templeman, Mr. P. Serjeants'-Inn
Templeman, Mrs. P.
Templeman, Mr. J.
Thackrack, J. Eſq.
Thomas, T. Eſq. *two copies*
Thomas, Freeman, Eſq. Chapel-Street, May-Fair
Thompſon, Rev. Mr.
Thompſon, Miſs
Tinney, Mr. John, Sarum
Tinting, Mr.
Titchborne, Sir Harry, Bart. *ſix copies*
Toghill, Rev. Mr. Chicheſter
Toke, Rev. W.
Tolley, Rev. Brownlow
Tomkyns, Rev. Mr. New college, Oxford, *four copies*
Tod, capt. James, Ocean Indiaman, *two copies*
Topping, Rev. Thomas, Blandford
Traverſe, Mr. Bridport
Tregonwell, Lewis, Eſq. *four copies*
Trenchard, Rev. George, Langton-Purbeck
Tripp, Henry, Eſq. Inner-Temple
Tripp, Rev. Mr. Rewe, Devon
Tripp, Miſs
Tripp, Miſs F.

Tripp, Mr. Petworth
Tripp, Rev. Dr.
Tripp, Mrs.
Tripp, Mrs.
Trift, Rev. Jeremiah, Verryan, Cornwall
Tucker, Mrs.
Turnor, Rev. Lewis
Turner, Mr.
Twopenny, Rev. Richard
Tyler, Mr.

U.

Upton, Mrs.
Valpy, Rev. R. F. A. S. Reading, Berks
Vanfittart, ——, Efq. New college, Oxford
Vaughan, ——, Efq.
Vernon, Mifs, *two copies*
Vernon, Mifs, Elizabeth
Vilett, Rev. Dr. *four copies*
Vyvyan, Richard, Efq. Exeter college, Oxford

W.

Wall, William, M. D. Oxford
Walker, Rev. Mr. Chichefter
Walker, Rev. Mr. New college, Oxford
Wallop, Hon. Mrs. Penton, Hants
Waller, Rev. Samuel, Steeple-Langford
Wanfey, Mrs. Sarum
Warton, Rev. Jofeph, D. D. Wickham, Hants
Warton, Mrs.
Warton, Mifs
Warton, Mrs. Jane, Wickham, Hants

Warton, Rev. Joseph, Tunworth, Hants
Warton, Mrs. Joseph
Warwick, Mrs. Walcot-Parade
Washington, Rev. Mr.
Waterford, Right Hon. Marquis of, Knt. St. Pk.
Watkins, Rev. Mr.
Watkins, Mrs.
Watkins, Mr. N.
Watson, John, Esq.
Watson, Mr. serjeant, Powis-Place
Webb, Mr.
Webber, Rev. C.
Weir, capt. Wickham, Hants
West, Rev. Dr.
Westcombe, Rev. Mr. Winchester
Wetherell, R. Esq. New college, Oxford
Whitaker, W. Esq. Shafton
Whitaker, Mr. New college, Oxford
Whightwich, Rev. H. fellow of Pembroke college, Oxford
Whalley, T. W. Esq.
Whalley, Mr.
White, Rev. J. fellow of New college, Oxford, *four copies*
White, Miss Mary, Sarum
White, Rev. William
White, Mr. John
Whitfield, Mr. J.
Wight, Rev. Osborne, *two copies*
Wilkinson, John, Esq.
Williams, Rev. Mr. fellow of Winchester college
Williams, ——, Esq. Southampton
Williams, James, Esq. Chettle, Dorset
Williamson, Mrs. Chapel-Street, Queen-Square, *two copies*
Wilmot, V. Henry, Esq.
Wilmot, Edward, Esq. Lansdown-Grove, Bath, *two copies*

Wilſon, capt. *four copies*
Willis, Rev. Thomas, Upper-Clatford
Willis, Rev. Francis, D.D. M.D.
Wiltſhire, John, Eſq. Bath
Woodgate, William, Eſq. Trinity college, Oxford
Wool, Rev. John, fellow of New college, Oxford
Woolſtonecraft, Edward Bland, Eſq.
Worceſter, Right Hon. Marquis of
Worſley, Mr. New college, Oxford
Wray, ——, Eſq. Southampton
Wright, William, Eſq. Drayton
Wyatt, Edgell, Eſq. Egham, Surry
Wyndham, H. P. Eſq. Sarum

Y.

Yeatman, Rev. John, Blandford
Yeo, William, Eſq.
Yeo, Mrs.
Yeomans, Rev. Mr. Wadham college, Oxford
Young, Rev. Mr. Birmingham

NAMES OMITTED.

Betteſworth, Mrs. Southampton
Rivers, Right Hon. Lord, *two copies*

xxvii

THE
COMPLAINT.

PENSIVE, and flow, with folitary steps
I trace the gardens wonted paths, by late
Remorfe, and impotent regret, compell'd
To ruminate on youthful follies, fad
Original of thoufand ills, of dire
Misfortune's baleful train th' unheeded fource:
Pale Poverty, whofe fpectre form attends
Sorrow and faded Care, and haughty Scorn
Of fterner afpect, and Unkindnefs harsh
The glance averting of her alter'd eye
At the dread nod of her terrific Queen;

Through the same ways my feet unguided bear

Me oft-returning, as the restless bird

Of summer, in repeated circles flies

With rapid wing, and panting fears to fix

Her claws adhesive on the grassy turf:

Thus circling move I with unequal pace,

Regardless of the never-ceasing hum

That fills my unattending ears; the laugh

Of playful children through the swarming street

In eager chase, and jocund merriment

Pursuing each the other; the loud peal

Of bells, to melody by neighb'ring stream

Soften'd from harshest tone, the rattling car,

And hoarser jarring of the pond'rous wain,

With all th' incessant din of busied trade.

Nor less unnotic'd is each rural sound

That strikes my once-enraptur'd ear, the song

Of whistling blackbird, the soft-cooing dove,

The bleat of ewe distress'd, that earnest calls

Her wanton young far wand'ring from her side

In heedless gambols through the neighb'ring mead.

In vain from yonder copse, whose boughs o'erhang

Stour's cavern'd banks, sad Philomel repeats

Her melancholy strain, with throat compress'd

Hoarse-gurgling now, and now with lengthen'd notes

Of still small sound preluding to a song

Of richest, thickly-warbled melody.

To other ears, sweet bird, address thy lay!

Thy strains, the sweet artificers of calm

Delight, and pensive pleasure, are of pow'r

To sooth to wish'd forgetfulness the cares

Of less afflicted mortals, whilst my mind

Brooding o'er mis'ry, dull to other sense,

Heeds not thy plaintive tale, thy tale of woes.

How light thy sorrows, when compar'd with mine!

But ah lefs tuneful my complaint, and rude

The cadence of my verfe; the mind opprefs'd

Builds not with fymmetry, and proportions due

The lofty rhyme, but oft in vain effays

To rife, by fpirit-damping cares weigh'd down,

As fickning bird that droops with moulting wing.

To thee unmindful of paft ills, a few

Short vernal funs, forgetfulnefs will bring

Of thy loft brood, and fond maternal hopes

To rear a fecond tuneful progeny.

To thee regardlefs of impending want

Each lonely dingle, and each hilly croft

Abundant food fupplies, where fwarming ants

People the black'ning hillocs earthy round.

For me, nor fleeting months, nor grateful change

Of feafons, in fucceffive order roll'd,

Nor fluctuating ebb of human things

A long-loft brother can reftore, or bid

Fond

Fond mem'ry from her living tablets raze
The manly virtues, gracefully severe,
That high exalted his aspiring soul
Above the vulgar herd; yet gentler oft
Their native firmness would relax, 'mid souls
Congenial, and in social converse mild,
Disclose each rare endowment, Attic wit
Temper'd by stronger sense, and copious stores
Of classic lore, harmoniously commix'd
With genuine thought, and knowledge underiv'd.
Nor seldom would he with a master's hand
Strike to bold chords the lyric shell, or pour
In freedom unrestrain'd the flowing rhyme.*

O early-lost farewell! th' officious muse
True to affection's call, would duly pay

* See the following Poem, entitled " The Pyramids of Egypt."

To thy lov'd shade, the well-deserved meed

Of tuneful tears, but that the icy hand

Of poverty with numbing influence choak

Chill'd inspiration's half-extinguished flame.

Fain would she sing how Itchen parent-stream

Struck with deep sorrow, check'd his murm'ring waves

Too eager haste; whilst on his banks he view'd

Thy length'ning fun'ral's melancholy pomp

In solemn, measur'd paces, flowly move.

Fain would she sing, how to old Ocean's court

The god repairing, 'mid th' assembled train

Of kindred deities, in speech abrupt

His fatal message told, th' untimely fate

Of him, his luckless favorite, which heard,

Sudden fair Isis, mute with sorrow, droops,

And from his chrystal throne, astonish'd Thames

Leaps, and with eager violence dashes down

His coral sceptre on the azure floor.

Him

Him weeps the goddefs of her tuneful fons
The firft, the chiefeft, him, the god who erft
In Latian ftrains of manlieft energy
Loud fung the praife of his majeftic ftream.*

Yet ftill, though quench'd her native flame, the mufe
Upheld by Patience, and her fifter bland
Calm Refignation, can with pious zeal
Kifs the afflictive rod, and though opprefs'd
With fruitlefs anguifh, impotent regret,
Can blefs the gracious pow'r that gives, nor blame
The hand that takes away; fond thought! perhaps
Left the drear profpect of the ills that wait
A brother's houfe, fhould with too keen a fting
His wakeful fenfe of woes fraternal wound.
Still does fhe feem, though rev'rend awe reftrain

---

* See the Latin Poem entitled "Rex Fluviorum Thamefis."

Her ken inquisitive, to view conceal'd
Beneath each just dispose of heav'n, some wise,
Some merciful intent, some real good
Unhop'd for, springing from imagin'd ill.
Still, though the sacrifice of scorn, she tread
This vale of tears with poverty her guide,
Yet arm'd with holy courage can she frame
Her meek petition thus " Thou gracious pow'r
" Parent of good, omniscient Lord, accept
" Thy lowly servant's grateful thanks, how due!
" For that thy tender and paternal care
" Of human frailty mindful, and the charm
" Of unresisted wealth, hath kindly plac'd
" The least, the lowest of thy worshippers
" In poverty's secure, though barren shade.
" O may my feeble virtue, impotent
" Of good, but for thy timely aid, derive
" New strength from thy due chastisement, nor sink

" In

" In blank dejection fpiritlefs, though clouds
" Of gath'ring woe impend; but rather taught
" Affliction's wifdom-giving lore, fubdue
" Wild paffion's clam'rous train, that vanquifh'd yield
" To moderation's fway th' ufurped breaft;
" And calm'd by charity, meek, chriftian grace,
" In paffive patience bear th' unheeded taunts
" Of fcornful pride, th' oppreffive violence
" Of wrefted law, the lofs of former fame,
" With all the accumulated ills that ftill
" Th' unenvied haunts of poverty attend."

THE

THE PYRAMIDS OF ÆGYPT,

Written in the year 1771, at Winchester College, by the late Reverend Thomas Warton, of New College, Oxford.

QUEEN of the east, whose penetrating mind
Disclos'd the light of science to mankind;
Who gave each arts' fair offspring to arise,
Who taught Astronomy to wing the skies,
Where Property and Order first began,
And sacred Law, chief excellence of man;
How art thou fall'n! thy glories, Ægypt, fled,
Thy sons of wisdom sunk among the dead!

But

But still aspires yon structure's cloud-capt height,
O'er Cairo's turrets less'ning to the sight:
Still does the Arab wild, who wanders nigh,
Search for the well-known top with weary eye.
High, as old Sangar crown'd with waving woods,
(The father he of Nilus' thund'ring floods)
Lifts to the nearer stars his pine-clad brow,
And frowns upon the humble cliffs below:
So yon aerial pile, whose topmost stone
(Where hovers round the stork with clam'rous moan,
And fears to place so high her infant brood)
Is rough with antique charms, and numbers rude;
Such as could cause Nile's constant stream to fail,
Such as could strip Behemoth's iron mail,
Such as could blast the hope of Ægypt's land,
Or plant the fig-tree in the burning sand,
Such as could desart make Osiris' dome,
Or fix the tented Arab to an home.

Scarce

Scarce on the top is heard the well-known song,
And bell, which leads the merchant train along,
While camels, rich with many a foreign bale,
Wind flowly trooping up the echoing vale.
Scarce can you view beneath the failor's toil,
And sheeted masts that whiten all the Nile;
Scarce can you hear the din of loud resort,
And busy murmurs of the crouded port,

But what avails the pomp of regal state?
The pride of art so impotently great?
Did nation then with foreign nation join,
And half the world to aid this work combine,
That the swath'd ghosts of Kings of ancient race,
Might sweep along these walls in ampler space?
That foul corruption 'mid this pomp might reign,
And feast in pillar'd halls her crawling train?

Britannia!

Britannia! think of Ægypt, and of Rome,
Nor lift for luxury the high-roof'd dome:
Let charity her fav'ring pinions spread
O'er ev'ry rising structure's tow'ring head;
Let age ne'er curse thy building's useless state,
Let want sit smiling at each palace gate;
So shall thy glory stand to future days,
And ev'ry Briton rival Wickham's praise.

REX

REX FLUVIORUM THAMESIS,

Auctore Thomâ Warton, 1772.

[This Poem obtained the annual Prize-Medal at Winchester College in the year 1772.]

UNDARUM venerande Pater, qui sternis inanem
Majestate gravi fremitum, & tacito agmine pergis,
Ito, fretis effunde tibi quas Anglia læta
Credit opes, tardoque advolvere in æquora fluctu!
Ite, O Naiades, nam vestras Thamesis undas
Ipse vocat faciles Genitor, fluviosque sequaces,
Ite choro propero peramabile plaudite littus,
Divæ, qua circum naturæ dædalus Ordo
Panditur, & rerum variarum oblectat imago.

Jactet

Jactet olivetum licet atque cacumen Hymetti
Iliffus, licet oftendat convallis honores
Peneus infignis, regalefque irriget hortos
Flumine felici Tigris, tua, Sequana, rura,
Et vineta colat fautor dilecta Lyæus;
Pulchrior Iliffo hic Fluvius, potioraque Tempe,
Flaventefque agri Pæftana rofaria vincunt
Et nitidas jactant quas Gallica littora vites.

O quis me ponat fublimi in vertice collis
Surgit ubi clivo molli Richmondia, & æquor
Subjectum afpectat, circum undique florea rura
Templaque confurgunt, lateque patentia culta,
Et Sylvarum umbræ vario difcrimine fparfæ
Per campos, armenta inter, divifaque agrorum
Meffis; nativo medius finuamine lapfus
Littoreas falices, & tecta propinqua domorum

                                              Riparum

Riparum villas oftentat latior amnis,
Dum tremulis undis adverfo fole relucet;

Hic olim veteres, Regalis fæva Tyranni
Sceptra indignati, Montanis arcibus agmen
Conjuratorum procerum, & focia arma vocantes,
Jus libertatis facrum, fædufque colendum
Firmarunt, Britones ; vidifti figna fecuta
Criftatofque duces, vidifti in margine ripæ,
Dum lætus tacitas preffifti Thamefis undas,
Affixum marmor, circum et fufpenfa Tropæa.
Extat adhuc faxum, monumentum immane, fuperftes,
Infignit memoremque locum paƈtumque notandum.
Contra ubi teƈta fpecus pendentia pumice vivo,
Et Tophos pandit nativos, fila Popeius
Suavia percurrens, mufas in vota vocavit,
Argumentum ingens reputans, & digna camænâ
Nomina, te Pater alme, tuoque in littore fylvas

Vinfo-

Vinforias celebrans, turriti et culmina tecti,

Culmina, quæ quondam mirandâ infigniit arte

Wiccamus Pater, antiqui monumenta laboris.

Salve! fancta domus Regum, tuque Aula verenda

Heroum mater falveto, ubi in ordine longo

Infignem comitatum Equites, Edvardus in armis

Conjunxit, dum fcuto atro, triplicique, decora

Exuviis Galli, plumâ, fe regia agebat

Digna Patrum victor foboles ante ora parentis.

Majori affurgas æftu, majora fluenta

Devolvas, Rex Undarum, qua Augufta fuperbam

Infigit fedem, ripamque accingit utramque

Turribus, Urbs Regina Orbis; quæ quantaque moles

Fluctibus infertur, connectenfque arcubus arcus,

Defpicit illifafque undas & vana frementes.

Afpice, ut innumeris albefcunt littora velis,

Innumeris remis vada fervent, inclytus auro
Plata, tibi cedros onerat, nativaque Volgam
Innatat altum abies, tibi, Flumen, ferica Ganges
Dat vexilla notis fluitare, et Turca, tiarâ
Submifsâ, veftras turres miratur, & ædem
Antiquam Petri, Medinæque æmula bufta,
Heroum facras defixus fufpicit urnas.

Illuftres Regum manes, Umbræque verendæ
Auguftam incolitis quæ fedem, Audite, fepultis
Si qua manet patriæ pietas, audite, nepotum
Emeritas laudes, ut veftra Britannia, tanta
Vertice fublimi gentes fupereminet omnes,
Quantus in Oceani Genitoris Thamefis aulâ
Urnam majorem oftendens, & plura tropæa
Contemnit divos alios, turbamque minorem.

PART OF THE FIRST BOOK

OF THE

ARGONAUTICS

OF

APOLLONIUS RHODIUS.

PHŒBUS inspire my song, while I resound
The deeds of men, in days of yore renown'd,
That o'er rough Pontus to the Phasian shores
Urg'd the swift Argo with unwearied oars;
And by stern Pelias sent, restor'd to Greece
The radiant honors of the golden fleece.

For thus, O Phœbus, from the Delphic cell
Thrice Pelias heard thee Fate's decree foretel,

" A stran-

" A stranger, with one foot unshod and bare,
" Shall soon arrive—Of him, O King, beware."
Thus spoke the god; when Jason pass'd the plains,
Where roar'd Anaurus swoll'n with wintry rains,
And as he strove to ford th' indignant flood,
Sudden immerg'd beneath the rising mud,
Each shoe forsook his feet—with one regain'd
He hastes to Pelias' hall—so Fate ordain'd;
He hastes the solemn festal rites to share
Which Pelias then (and such his annual care)
To Neptune chief, and all th' immortals paid,
Yet still was Argive Juno disobey'd.
Instant the King, as Jason met his eyes,
" Lo! this the man decreed by Phœbus," cries:
Then strait, th' impending danger to prevent,
To distant seas and shores the youth he sent,
To strive with shipwrecks on the watry way,
Or fall to savage men an helpless prey.

Fame

Fame oft has told how Argus' dædal hand
Rear'd the huge frame, that bore the val'rous band.
Be mine the birth of each, and toils, to sing;
Ye Mufes all your aid propitious, bring!
With Orpheus' facred name begin the fong,
Whom, fweeteft fifter of the tuneful throng,
Calliope, to brave Æagrus bore
Where fteep Parnaffus rears his forefts hoar.
He bent the ftubborn cliffs by mufic's force,
His verfe could tame the torrent's headlong courfe.
Ev'n now the fhore of Thracian Zone along,
Fair monuments of his prevailing fong.
Tall, fpreading beeches wave in verdant row,
Drawn by his harp, from Pindus' neighb'ring brow.
Him, King of Thrace, the partner of his woes,
As Chiron fagely counfell'd, Jafon chofe.
And next, for whom his Sire Cometes tri'd
Love's joys on proud Apidnus' fruitful fide,

(There,

(There, where his streams, vast regions wander'd o'er,
Pour on Enipeus' tides in horrid roar)
Asterion, 'mid the chiefs enroll'd his name;
To him succeeds the mighty Polypheme;
Larissa's glitt'ring tow'rs his fam'd abode,
Who, when with youthful heat his bosom glow'd,
Shone 'mid the Lapithæ in conqu'ring arms
To quell th' invading Centaurs loud alarms.
Though now cold age his fainting frame opprefs'd,
Yet still the martial spirit warm'd his breast.
Nor long in native Phylace detain'd
Uncle of Jason, Iphitus remain'd.
He joins the band by ties domestic led,
His blooming sister shar'd old Æson's bed.
Admetus too forsook his spreading flocks,
And pastures bord'ring fair Chalcydon's rocks.
And next, who boast the son of May their Sire,
Their mother Menetus Antianire,

With

With Echion, Erytus adorn the band
Skill'd in their father's fly deceit of hand.
To these soft-tongued Æthalides succeeds
Their brother, whom beneath the whisp'ring reeds
That thinly shade Amphryssus' winding shore,
The martial Myrmidonian Pthias bore.
With these advanc'd from Gyrto's lofty seats
Coronus tried in war, and manly feats,
Yet was his Sire still fiercer in the fight
Who single turn'd the Centaur-train to flight;
Tho' soon the Centaur-train resum'd their rage,
Fac'd back, and dar'd th' invading chief engage.
But tho' nor steel his hardy limbs might gore,
From Pelion's sides the nodding pines they tore;
With these rush'd dreadful on, and buried deep
His yet unbroken limbs beneath the branching heap.
Next Mopsus came, whom Phœbus taught to sing
The flight of birds, and omens of the wing.

You too Eurydamas, your feat forsake
Where Thracian Xynias sleeps, a sullen lake.
And Actor rous'd his son, from Opoen's tow'rs
To gain new palms amid th' assembled pow'rs.
Then haste Eurytion and Erybote,
Of Actor this, of Teleon that begot.
With these Oileus skill'd or to oppose
Or chase in headlong flight the trembling foes.
And Canthus mingled in the val'rous train
Sent by Canethus from th' Eubæan plain,
But brave, and warm'd with glorious hopes in vain.
Ev'n now th' unerring Fates foretold his doom
Ev'n now they destin'd him an early tomb,
(With Mopsus, skilful of prophetic lore)
Far off on Lybia's solitary shore.
From Cholcis far, as from the western way
In orient glory dawns the god of day.

And

And next proud regents of th' Æchalian land,

Clytius, and Iphitus encreaſe the band;

Their Sire ſtern Erytus, the Bowyer-god

On whom his quiver'd ſtores and bow beſtow'd;

But ſoon the chief (ah ill-requited gift)

Dar'd his own arms, againſt the god to lift.

Nor ſhall th' Æacidæ be loſt to fame

Diff'rent their cities, tho' their birth the ſame:

For ſince in evil hour, and angry mood

They dar'd to dip their hands in brother's blood,

Beneath their guilty ſteel ſince Phocus bled,

Far from Ægina's native tow'rs they fled.

You, Telamon, in Atthis fix'd your ſeat,

Pthias to Peleus gave a ſafe retreat.

Nor martial Butes, from Cecropia's plain

Bold Teleon's offspring, ſhall unſung remain.

And

And brave Phalerus' name shall deck my page,
The blossom of his Sire's declining age:
Yet tho' this son alone remain'd to shed
The balm of comfort o'er his hoary head;
Tho' blossom of his age, from his lov'd side,
Far off he sent the boy to stem the stormy tide.
Meantime, the bravest of the Athenian train
Thesus was held, in Pluto's heavy chain.
Since for Pirithous, his slaughter'd friend,
He dar'd to hell's dark passages descend.
Else both in Jason's aid had deign'd to rise,
And made the beamy fleece an easier prize.

Typhis Agniades shall next be sung,
From the Siphæan tribe in Thespia sprung.
'Twas his the future tempest to foretel,
And when the billowy plains would sink or swell.

'Twas

'Twas his, as fun or ſtars gave ſign to guide

The murm'ring prow ſecure along the tide.

A welcome chief, amid' th' heroic band

He claim'd a place at Pallas' high command,

Pallas who lent to Argus ſkill divine,

And taught the ſage to ſhape the Pelian pine,

Than which no ſhip amid' the watry roar

Mov'd more obedient to the ſtruggling oar.

Then Phlias march'd from Erythreas' tow'rs

His fable fountain where Aſopus pours.

With theſe be, Talaus, thy name enroll'd,

Areius and Leodocus the bold.

Argos their feat, and Bias was their Sire,

With Neleis Pero mix'd in ſoft deſire.

For whom within Iphiclus' plenteous ſtall

Long time Melampus groan'd in weary thrall.

Nor now could Hercules inactive ſleep

While all with mutual ardor fought the deep.

Soon

Soon as it ſtruck th' exulting hero's ear
How preſs'd the gallant chiefs from far and near,
Sudden his haſty feet retrod the plain,
O'er which conſtrain'd in many a maſſy chain,
He bore the ſavage of Lampeia's wood
That waves o'er Erymanthus' ſedgy flood.
Which 'mid Mycenæ's chiefs aſſembled round
His huge hands heav'd ſcarce ſtruggling to the ground.
Sudden he haſtes as glory warm'd his breaſt,
Nor urg'd by fell Euryſtheus' dire beheſt,
To meet th' aſſembled pow'rs :—beneath his ſide
Hylas appears, in youth's freſh-ſpringing pride.
Hylas the conſtant partner of his care
And faithful ſtill his darts and bow to bear.
With theſe was Nauplius ſeen in arms to ſhine
Nauplius the ſeed of Danaus divine.
Nauplius in naval arts by none outvied
That occupied their buſineſs on the tide.

By

By Danais Amymone disclos'd to birth,
His Sire the god that shakes the solid earth.
Last of the chiefs that Argos turrets boast
Idmon was added to th' advent'rous host;
Tho' 'mid that host the chief his death foretold,
Skill'd in the lots that Fate's dark volumes hold;
Yet still to shun the coward's hated name
He gave his life, a forfeit prize for fame:
Nor he, as fame reports, of Abas born
But of the god, that gives ambrosial morn.
By him inspir'd, the sage could well divine
From flight of birds, and each refulgent sign.
With Jason next to gain of fame the meed
Pollux the tamer of the fiery steed,
And Castor on victorious deeds intent
From Sparta's lofty turrets Leda sent.
Their birth divine how better could they prove
What task more glorious for the sons of Jove?

And

And next their limbs with might prodigious brac'd,
Lynceus and Idas from Arena haste;
Nor so renown'd was Lynceus' hardy might,
As the keen vigour of his piercing sight,
Which, if tradition fables not, survey'd
Thro' earth's deep centre hell's sequester'd shade.
You too, Periclymene, the train adorn
Eldest of Neleus' sons in Pylos born,
Thee Neptune taught in dangers of the fight
To shift at will thy shape, and cheat the sight.
Nor thou to speak the names, benignant Muse,
Of Cepheus, and Amphidamas refuse,
Aleus their Sire, and on th' Arcadian plain
Their proud inheritance Apheidas' reign.
With Tegeas' tow'rs, Ancæus these attends
Their eldest brother, whom Lycurgus sends.
Himself the part of filial duty chose
To cheer his hoary father's soft repose.

The

The youth, undeck'd with steel's resplendent pride,
Wore of a savage boar the horrid hide,
On Mænalus o'ershadow'd summits slain;
His hands a two-edg'd battle-ax sustain,
For cautious to detain him safe at home,
Within the lofty castle's inmost dome,
(Vain stratagem, the breast when glory warms)
Aleus conceal'd the stripling's radiant arms.

Then lame Augæas boastful of his Sire
The god that rolls, bright Heav'ns diurnal fire,
Fir'd with ideas of the Colchian land
He left o'er Eleas' tow'rs his wide command,
Eager the Scythian tyrant to behold
He left his shining heaps of treasur'd gold.

And next from val'rous Hyperasius sprung
Amphion, and Asterius shall be sung;
Their seat Pellene fair, which Pallas plac'd
Where the scoop'd shores resist the watry waste.

Next

Next Polypheme from Tænarus sublime
Eager advanc'd the wond'rous bark to climb;
Well was he skill'd in airy course to sweep
O'er the blue surface of the level deep;
And as the watry passage he pursued,
Scarce his suspended feet the brine bedew'd.
Brave Tytius' daughter whom Europa gave
To birth; his Sire, the god that rules the wave.
And next, who Neptune's sacred lineage boast
Ancæus and Erginus join the host;
This from the tow'rs that bear Miletus' name,
From Samos, that, where Juno's altars flame;
Or skill'd to guide the vessel o'er the main,
Or urge the thunder of th' embattled plain.
The glorious conq'ror of the monstrous boar,
Next Meleager leaves th' Ætolian shore;
Æneus his Sire, and Æneus' brother came
Laocoon, yet not their birth the same,
His mother was a mercenary dame.

'Twas

'Twas his with precepts mild of sapient age,

To guide his youthful nephew's headlong rage.

But had that youth within his native land

Told one year longer, ere he join'd the band

O'er all his virtues had superior shone,

Excell'd by godlike Hercules alone.

To him succeeds Iphiclus in the rear

Skill'd with unerring arm to launch the spear.

Or o'er the level green with winged pace

To bound the foremost in the rapid race.

Next Palæmonius, Lernus' offspring brave,

His aid with zealous pride to Jason gave.

Lernus his name, but Vulcan was his race,

For with one foot he limp'd an awkward pace.

Yet strong besides, and beauteous was his frame,

And fir'd his breast with valour's genuine flame.

The son of Naubolus next honour warms

Phocensian Iphitus to shine in arms:

Brave

Brave Jason's hoſt, what time from Pythos' fane
Phœbus foretold his dangers on the main.
Zetes, and Calais, next the heroes join
Of winged Boreas, the ſons divine,
Who ſhar'd in Orithûias' fierce embrace
Far in the frozen bounds of wintry Thrace.
For as the feſtal dance the virgin led
O'er the green banks by fair Iliſſus fed,
The god beheld her, and, enamour'd, bore
Far off to bleak Erginus founding ſhore,
And where Sarpedon's tow'ring ſummits riſe
Heaving to Heav'n his cliffs of horrid ice,
Bade riſe around a ſable mantling cloud
From mortal view their mutual joys to ſhroud.
Each chief with ſwiftneſs more than mortal ſprings
And ſhakes on either feet his gloomy wings;
Which to the ſun (cœleſtial ſight) unfold
Gay-glancing ſcales that blaze with burniſh'd gold;

         While

While down their backs a sheet of azure hair
Rolls in redundant curls, and floats abroad in air.

Nor now th' indulgence of domestic ease
Detain'd Acastus from the stormy seas.
Nor Argus was away, whose dædal hand
Well knew to frame the works which Pallas plann'd.

Such were the chiefs in Jason's cause who came,
Whom all around the Minyan noble's name
For all the bravest of the chosen host,
Their high descent from Minyas' daughters boast:
From Minyas sprung the beauteous Alcimede
Bore the brave chief, the val'rous train who led.

Now stood the ship in all her fair array
Complete, and furnish'd for the watry way:

The Princes haſte to the Magneſian ſtrand
Where, Pagaſæ, thy far-fam'd ſummits ſtand;
And as around them preſs the thick'ning crouds
Blaze forth like ſilver ſtars, from ſable clouds.
All on their dazzling arms in ſilence gaze
Awhile; then thus diſcloſe their deep amaze.
" Eternal Jove! what unforeſeen alarm!
" Say, why ſhould Greece her braveſt warriors arm?
" This pomp of war, Oh whither can ſhe ſend?
" Or what can Pelias' dark deſigns intend.
" Unleſs Æetes reconcil'd to peace
" To yon brave hoſt reſign the radiant fleece;
" One day ſhall ſee the tyrant's ſtately ſpires
" Smoke on the ground enwrapp'd in Grecian fires.
" If thou, great Jove, but ſmooth the Pontic tide
" And bid for Jaſon ev'ry ſtorm ſubſide."

Meantime the matrons for their ſafe return
Prefer the pray'r, the ſteaming incenſe burn;

Nor

Nor was their woe for Alcimede opprefs'd,

While each her lov'd affociate thus addrefs'd:

" Comes them at laft misfortune's dreary ftorm

" Thy life's unclouded evening to deform?

" Sad Alcimede! and do the Fates deny

" Thine years to fet, in mild ferenity;

" But doubly, Æfon, is thy woe fevere

" Far better born upon the fable bier,

" Thine aged limbs had flept in earth's cold womb,

" Ere thou hadft known thy Jafon's dreary doom.

" Oh had the radiant ram when Helle died

" With Phrixus whelm'd beneath the clofing tide

" Ne'er liv'd in human accents to difclofe

" The dark decrees of fate, and future woes."

And next of various fex, and various years,

Amid her weeping flaves, the Queen appears,

While Æfon funk in languor as he lies

Bedews the bed of age with all a father's eyes,

But Jason strives their unavailing woes
With balmy words of comfort to compose,
And bids th' assistants to the sounding shore
Of well-tried weapons waft an ample store;
In silent grief th' assistant train obey,
And, weeping, to the vessel take their way.
But Alcimede, with woe superior stung,
Round Jason's neck in fond embraces hung;
The Virgin thus whom cruel fate detain
Baneath some rig'rous step-dame's tedious chain,
(Who each sad day with harsh ungentle sounds,
And taunts severe her meeker nature wounds,)
To sooth the sadness of her state forlorn
With her hoar-tressed nurse is seen to mourn:
Around her well-known neck her arms she throws,
And scarce for sighs can the big grief disclose.
Thus, as in close embrace she clasp'd her son,
Her sorrowing plaint had Alcimede begun:

       " Unhappy

" Unhappy Queen ! Oh had thy limbs been laid

" Long since in dark oblivion's silent shade,

" From life at once and sorrow's anguish freed,

" When Pelias thy sad distiny decreed.

" Then thy dear hands my languid eyes had clos'd,

" And in the tomb my breathless corse compos'd.

" This only office of thy filial care

" Thy wretched mother fondly hop'd to share.

" Ah what avails, that each Thessalian dame

" Once heard with duteous awe my lofty name,

" If joyless through my desolated dome

" I like a captive maid am doom'd to roam !

" Since all that lofty name I once could boast,

" And all my glories are in Jason lost !

" For thee I first and last unloos'd the zone,

" For thee I felt Lucina's pangs alone.

" O unexpected stroke ! undreamt-of blow !

" That Phrixus' flight should prove the source of woe !"

Thus wept the Queen, th' attendant train receive
Her loud laments, and struck with mutual sorrow grieve,
When Jason thus his prudent speech address'd,
" Add not new griefs to this distracted breast;
" For wretched mortals righteous Jove prepares
" A still-successive train of weary cares;
" Yet, Oh my mother, let it sooth thy grief
" That Pallas lends thy son her sage relief,
" That lucky signs are giv'n from Phœbus shrine
" And all the flow'r of valiant Greece is mine:
" Do thou retir'd, with this thy faithful train,
" Peaceful at home, in calm repose, remain;
" Yet Oh restrain thy unavailing tears,
" Nor thus, divine of ill, awake our fears!"

He spoke, and trod with loftier pace along,
Thick, and more thick, advance the eager throng:

As

As when Apollo leaves his fragrant ſhrine

Within his native Delos, iſle divine,

Or from proud Claros, or from Delphos moves

Or Xanthus ſtreams that lave wide Lycia's groves:

So mov'd great Jaſon, through the yielding croud,

The many rend the ſkies with plaudits loud.

Iphias, by duty urg'd, though bent with age

(Of guardian Artemis the Prieſtefs ſage)

With feeble ſteps, ſcarce ſtruggles thro' the band

To kiſs the parting heroes holy hand.

Much would ſhe ſay, but unreſtrain'd and rude

On the ſhort interview the crouds intrude;

And urging with refiſtleſs force aſide

The weeping Matron from the chief divide.

Now reach his ſteps the Pagaſæan ſtrand
Where lodg'd in Argo wait the godlike band.

He

He mounts her lofty sides, in order'd rows

The chiefs fall back, and one deep file compose.

Now from the town advancing to the bay

Argus, and young Acastus, they survey:

Yet came they not, as will'd their haughty Sire,

But mad for fame, and fill'd with votive fire.

Argus in many a dreadful fold unfurls

A bull's rough hide o'erspread with sable curls;

Adown his mighty limbs, embroider'd o'er

With dædal hand, a vest Acastus wore,

Which erst his sister Pelopea wove,

And gave her brother, monument of love.

Meantime, lest every tongue with varied sound

Of earnest questions order should confound,

A solemn council, thro' th' obedient band

Is held in state at Jason's high command:

Some on the cordage and the sails are plac'd

Some take their seats, along the prostrate mast.

         When

When Jason thus addrefs'd th' affembled train,

" Whate'er may fit our veffel for the main,

" Or deck, or guard us, through the watry road

" Is duly, O my bounteous friends, beſtow'd.

" Then why delay to bid th' unfurled fail

" Wait the firſt whiſpers of the profp'rous gale.

" Yet Oh fince all one common caufe unite

" One toil to ſtem the ſtormy feas invite;

" All to fubdue the proud Æetes burn

" All wifh to native Greece, a fafe return:

" Ere yet we part, leſt future conteſts rife,

" Some gallant leader of our enterprife,

" With caution chufe; or in the ſtern debate

" To guide th' embattled bands, with mind fedate;

" Or if the Scythian King to peace incline

" In holy league the plighted hand to join."

He fpoke; on Hercules with one confent

Silent awhile their eager eyes they bent,

As

As in the midst he sat, then loudly cried,

" Be gallant Hercules, our godlike guide."

Stern from his seat, he thus address'd the band,

As all aloft he waves his mighty hand:

" To me a task too glorious is decreed;

" That chief alone th' assembled troops shall lead,

" Who first conven'd us, urg'd by warmer zeal:

" Who dares deny Alcides' rage shall feel."

He spoke, around approving clamours ran;

Then Jason rose, and joyful thus began:

" Since with united voice, my friends, ye deign

" That I conduct your labours o'er the main,

" Lest ought retard us in the dang'rous way

" Our festal rites to Phœbus first we'll pay:

" And whilst my swains select of fairest hue

" Victims to deck the feast with honour due;

" Our-

" Ourselves will heave the vessel from the shores
" Dispose the seats, adjust th' allotted oars:
" Then sacred to th' Embasian pow'r divine
" Our hands along the beach shall rear a shrine;
" Who promis'd to direct our path aright,
" And ope old Ocean to my piercing sight.
" If ere my contest with the Colchian Lord,
" His aid were first in sacred rites implor'd."

He spoke, and to the toil his hands address'd
His great example kindling ev'ry breast:
They bare their limbs, their vests a radiant heap
Are thrown in haste upon a rocky steep
That o'er the sea's retreating surface rose,
Yet recent from the wave, and wet with ooze.
On either side, the naval armament
Duly they place on Argus' voice intent;

The

The stores in happiest regulation place
The piny texture more completely brace;
The looser planks with nails tenacious bind,
So shall her sides outbrave the rushing wind:
Then dig a trench, as Argo long and wide,
Whence to the waves descending she might glide,
Equal at first, the end with gradual sweep
Sunk deeper, reach'd the hoarse-resounding deep:
To this adapted in due-order'd rows
Beneath the keel, smooth leavers they dispose,
That when the first were touch'd, without delay
She o'er the rest might win her easy way:
Then to the thongs their oars inverted bound
On either side, and form two ranks around:
To these their hands, and hardy breasts apply,
Tiphys applauds the toil with cheering cry.
Eager they rush with hands, and breasts conjoin'd
And still a firmer footing seem to find:

Bursts

Bursts from the trench the huge reluctant frame,

The striving heroes pour the loud acclaim.

Groan'd the stretch'd leavers, the vast keel beneath,

Issues the smoke in many a darksome wreath.

With crashing sound she shoots into the main,

The chiefs with skill her farther course restrain;

Then make their oars in the smooth sockets fast,

And in the midship rear the spiry mast.

Then as the shaken lots their seats dispose

By pairs the heroes fill succeffive rows;

Yet in the midst, a more distinguish'd space,

Ancæus Tegeas pow'rful King they place

With godlike Hercules, to these alone

As of superior rank was favour shown.

But to brave Tiphys as of skill well-tried,

They gave the vessel's doubtful helm to guide.

Then of rude stones, that form'd the craggy shore,

The wand'ring chiefs collect an ample store;

Of

Of these devoted to th' Epactian name
Of great Embasius, an high altar frame;
And on its top by rites paternal led
A fading olive's leafless branches spread.

Meantime, the swains as Jason gave command,
Conduct the victims to the winding strand;
The salted cake prepare, the lavers bring
Fill'd with pure water from the chrystal spring;
When thus in prostrate adoration laid
To Phœbus pow'r paternal, Jason pray'd:
" Hear, Pagasæan King, whose sacred sway
" My father Æson's lofty tow'rs obey,
(" And think that from thy own prophetic tongue
" This train of all my destin'd labours sprung)
" Do thou direct us to the wish'd-for fleece,
" And waft our ship again to native Greece.

" To

" To thee, for every chief whose safe return
" Thy pow'r shall grant, a votive bull shall burn;
" And many an off'ring hung aloft shall shine,
" Both at thy Pythian, and Ortygian shrine.
" Ere yet we sail, regard with fav'ring eyes
" This our first gift of solemn sacrifice.
" O pow'rful patron of th' unerring bow
" Ere yet we loose, some lucky omen show,
" If you but smile, each ruder storm shall sleep,
" And peace sit brooding o'er th' unruffled deep."

Thus pray'd the chief, and next in order due
The salted cake on Ocean's bosom threw;
While Hercules and bold Ancæus rise
To flay the victims for the sacrifice.
On this with headlong hand the son of Jove
Where rose the front, his club's huge burden drove;

Low sinks the beast beneath the knotty mass:
The brother-bull with battle-axe of brass
Ancæus smote; where tempting to the blade
Its ridgy length of brawn the neck display'd.
Spouts the black blood, the solid tendons burst,
Prone falling on his horns he ploughs the dust.
The limbs they sever from th' inclosing hide
The thighs selected to the gods divide,
On these in double caul involv'd with art,
The choicest morsels lay from every part,
Then on the cleft-wood place; the flames aspire
While Jason feeds with votive wine the fire.
Prophetic Idmon views with ravish'd eyes
The grateful steam o'er all the off'ring rise;
And as the curling volume he surveys,
The oracle of Phœbus thus displays:
" The fates indulgent give ye to restore
" The golden fleece to Grecia's native shore;

" Yet

" Yet ere your wifh'd return from favage foes,
" From tempefts, ye fhall feel unnumber'd woes.
" For me, fome lucklefs dæmon will ordain
" An early death, on Libya's lonely plain.
" This doom long fince has my pervading eye
" Learn'd from the leaves of dark futurity.
" Yet what if death my enterprife await,
" Be that, if glory crown my name, my fate."
He fpoke, attentive to the prophet's voice
The heroes for their fafe return rejoice:
Yet inly griev'd they, for th' untimely doom
Of Idmon deftin'd to an early tomb.

Now came mild eve, the golden orb of day
Haften'd to bath him in the weftern bay;
The tow'ring cliffs with verdant woods array'd
Projected o'er the plains a longer fhade.

With careful hands, the heroes on the shore,
Where from the sands retir'd the billows hoar,
Of high-heap'd leaves an ample couch compose,
There rest their mighty limbs in order'd rows.
In portion'd share rich viands smok'd around,
And luscious wine the copious goblets crown'd.
Then various talk among the chiefs arose
Such as from friendship's genial fountain flows;
From mutual intercourse of op'ning souls
When youthful breasts are warm'd with flowing bowls.
Meantime in solemn silence Jason sat
Revolving in his mind the will of fate:
Despair's dark clouds involve his musing brows,
While Ocean's wave, in thought, the hero ploughs.
Idas observ'd and thus with ill-tim'd rage,
" Jason what various thoughts, thy mind engage?
" Unless thy tongue by tardy fear be froze,
" The secret purpose of thy heart disclose.

" Dege-

' Degen'rate chief! and finks thy foul with fear?
" Now fwear I by this oft-victorious fpear,
" Idas will ne'er to death or danger yield,
" Though Jove himfelf fhould meet me in th' em-
    battled field.
" Lo Jafon fuch th' ally, whom glory calls
" To fight thy battles from Arena's walls."
He fpoke; and lifting drain'd the copious bowl
That fill'd with high-flown infolence his foul.
Through the whole train, tumultuous clamors ran,
Till Idmon thus his bold rebuke began:
" Rafh man, does wine fuch boaftful thoughts infpire
" And urge thee to provoke Heav'ns awful Sire?
" Thus, as tradition fays, th' Aleian pair
" Did impious war 'gainft matchlefs Jove declare.
" Yet they, though braver far than thee, funk low
" Smote by the archer-god's unerring bow."

He spoke; with scornful laugh, and gestures rude,
Proud Idas thus his taunting speech renew'd:
" Say, prophet, does thy father-god decree,
" As for th' Aleian twins, such death for me?
" Yet know, bold seer, if thy prophetic strain
" Falsely-inspir'd should prove thy threat'nings vain,
" Nor fraud, nor force oppos'd, shall e'er withstand
" The promis'd vengeance of my pow'rful hand."
Now sharper conflict and dire deeds of blood
Between th' impetuous heroes had ensued,
But that the chiefs, with threats and counsel sage,
As Jason order'd, check'd their rising rage.

Meantime, who best the passions could compose
With music's soothing accents, Orpheus rose:
In his left hand the silver-sounding strings
He rears, and thus the sweet musician sings:

In

In the beginning, how the earth, the deep,
The Heav'ns were in one tumultuous blended heap:
'Till nature parted the conflicting foes,
And beauteous order from confusion rose.
How ev'ry shining orb that nightly glows
O'er the blue vault, his place and order knows.
How silver Cynthia, and the golden sun,
Their radiant course by turns rejoice to run.
Whence rose the rocks with waving verdure crown'd,
From what vast source the rapid rivers found,
Whence sprung their nymphs, from what mysterious seed,
O'er earth's green bosom swarms the reptile breed.
And next the tuneful master shifts the strain
To old Ophion's dark primœval reign;
Who with his bride the daughter of the deep,
First claim'd the throne on hoar Olympus' steep:

'Till from their head a pow'r superior rent
The sacred badge of pow'r omnipotent;
On Saturn's head Ophion's honours plac'd,
And with his consort's glories Rhea grac'd:
Themselves were plung'd in Ocean's dark domain,
While Saturn rul'd the Titan's godlike train;
While Jove was young, and lull'd in infant rest,
The dark Dictæas sacred rock possess'd:
Ere his dread bolt the earth-born Cyclops fram'd,
Ere from the darken'd heav'ns the livid lightning flam'd.
This said th' immortal bard his lyre unstrung,
And stopp'd th' ambrosial music of his tongue:
Yet still the heroes with attentive ear
Thought him still singing, still stood fix'd to hear,
In silent rapture; tho' the bard had ceas'd,
Still on the dying murmurs seem'd to feast.

Now

Now Cynthia's star-encircled orb arose,
The drooping heroes sink in soft repose:
But when the bright-eyed morning's purple rays
O'er Pelion's redd'ning pines began to blaze,
And ebbing waves by cooling breezes fann'd
In gentle heavings broke upon the strand;
Then warn'd by Tiphys' voice they leave the shores,
Climb the tall ship and grasp their order'd oars.

Now with portentous roaring all around
The winding Pagasæan bays resound.
Impatient Argo the glad signal took,
While from her vocal keel loud murmurs broke,
Her keel by Pallas fram'd from Dodonæan oak.
Now ranging each their arms in martial state,
In order'd rows the daring heroes sat.
Yet still Ancæus of Neptunian race
By gen'ral suffrage held the middle place.

With

With him Alcides' giant-strength was join'd,
Inactive by his side his club reclin'd.
While as he takes his seat, beneath the load
The keel subsides opprefs'd, and feels the demi-god.
Their haulsers now they loose; and o'er the brine
Pour the rich off'ring of nectareous wine.
While Jason, as the bay swift Argo leaves,
Looks back on Grecia's shores, and silent grieves.
As to the warbles of the sacred lyre
The blooming youths, Apollo's festive choir,
Or in the Delphian, or the Delian fane,
Or where Ismenus feeds the fertile plain,
The sacred altars blazing flame around
In spritely dance and order'd measure bound;
So Argo's heroes, as the seas they swept,
To Orpheus' harp according measure kept.

SOLITUDE

AT AN INN.

OFT upon the twilight plain
Circled with thy fhadowy train,
While the dove at diftance coo'd,
Have I met thee, Solitude!
Then was lonelinefs to me
Beft, and true fociety.
But, ah! how alter'd is thy mein
In this drear, deferted fcene!
Here thou com'ft in fullen mood,
Not with thy fantaftic brood
Of beck'ning fhapes, and vifions airy
Summon'd from the land of Fairy.

Here

Here all thy wonted pleasures cease,

Musing, mild, and pensive peace :

No poetic being here

Strikes with whisper'd sound mine ear.

No converse here, to fancy cold,

With many a fleeting form I hold.

Here all inelegant and rude

Is thy form, sweet Solitude !

EPITAPH.

HERE rests, within this narrow cell, a wife
Whose gentle manners sooth'd the cares of life:
Example rare of patience undismay'd
By the near prospect of death's awful shade:
In youth she fell: yet did she not complain
Or Heav'ns immutable decrees arraign:
But tremblingly rejoicing fix'd her eye
With stedfast hopes on immortality.

O may such hopes, so firm, such pious joy,
Such glorious views our latest hours employ!

TO A PAINTER.

IN vain, rash man, thy feeble colours trace
Each blooming beauty of Eliza's face:
The coral lip, and sweetly-smiling cheek
Where laughter loves to live in dimple sleek:
Those eyes, whence love renews his hallow'd fire
With brighter flames than kindle warm desire.

With equal hope my emulative song
Might praise the sweetness of her tuneful tongue,
Or sing her polish'd sense, and taste refin'd,
And milder graces of her gentle mind.
In this, howe'er, agree our faint essays,
So far her bloom exceeds thy pencil's praise
As her unrivall'd song my humbler lays.

FROM THE GREEK

OF

SIMONIDES.

WHEN now the cheft, by art Dœdalean join'd,
Was tofs'd by fwelling waves and adverfe wind,
With tearful eyes the wretched Danae caft
Her hands maternal round her infant's waift,
And thus, "What grief, my child, corrodes my breaft
" Whilft thou, like fated babes, enjoy'ft thy wonted reft!
" Dark is thy joylefs dwelling, dark as night,
" Save when the pale moon lends a doubtful light.
" Thou in thy purple mantle fleep'ft reclin'd,
" Nor heedeft ought the waves of fiercer wind;

" That

" That idly rage around thy darkſome bed,

" Nor wet the flowing hairs that deck thy infant head.

" Sweet babe, thou wouldſt, were theſe my ſorrows thine,

" Thy tender ear to my diſtreſs incline.

" Sleep on, (thy mother bids) winds ceaſe to blow!

" Sleep boiſt'rous waves, and ſleep my unexampled woe.

FROM THE GREEK

OF

APOLLONIUS RHODIUS.

Now night o'er earth her dark'ning vapours shed,
And the black deep a gradual shade o'erspread;
With upward eyes the mariners survey
Thy star Orion, and thine Helice;
Wrapp'd in deep sleep the wearied pilgrim lies,
And slumbers seal the o'erwatch'd porter's eyes;
Ev'n she at length forgets her griefs in rest
Whose babe deceas'd no longer craves her breast;
No dogs are heard throughout the city's bound,
No busy murmur, no tumultuous sound:
Silence and Darkness hold their equal reign
O'er crouded city, and o'er desart plain:

But fad Medea's eyes no reft can clofe,

For watchful cares have chas'd away repofe.

Still Jafon's form is prefent to her mind,

And dreadful lowings feem to fill each hollow wind

Of bulls, by whom the haplefs youth muft yield

To death untimely in the martial field:

A thoufand cares her panting bofom move,

She trembles now with fear, and now with love:

As when of folar beams the fplendors bright

Strike on the walls, with quick-reflected light,

From the full vafe, where late-infufed ftreams

From fparkling wave fhoot forth tranflucent beams;

Above, below, the glitt'ring fplendors dance

In circles fwift, and many-twinkling glance;

Thus various cares the virgin's bofom tear,

And anxious grief diftracts, and doubtful fear:

Now kind compaffion gives her tears to flow,

And her pale form confumes with inward woe.

Sharp,

Sharp, throbbing pains convulfe her beauteous head,
When now love's fiercer pow'r through her whole frame has fpread.
Now impotent of mind fhe vows to give
Her opiate drugs, the monfters to deceive;
Her purpofe now with fudden change foregoes,
And meditates in death to end her woes:
Anon nor death fhe feeks, nor will fhe quell
Th' unconquerable bulls with magic fpell,
But vainly hopes, forgetting, and forgot,
To bear in filent wretchednefs her lot.

A

SACRED ANACREONTIC

O D E.

LIFT, my soul, thy thoughts above
Wine and mirth and guilty love;
To sublimer themes aspire,
Change the tender Teiian lyre;
With a louder, alter'd string
Praise creation's bounteous King,
In the dulcet Dorian mood
Boldly strive to hymn thy God.
Who his matchless acts can count?
Mercy's inexhaustless fount!

View below, about, above
Steps of wisdom, pow'r, and love.

While my votive lyre I sweep,
Nature, solemn silence keep!
Furious winds, your roarings cease,
Floods, and dashing torrents, peace!
Herds, from echoing hill, to hill,
Warblers of the woods, be still!
On this praise-devoted day
Let the lion spare his prey!
Let no poison-bloated snake
Scare the pilgrim from the brake;
Let not impious war assail
The peaceful shepherd's silent vale.

How with weights of wonder press'd
Shall I ease my throbbing breast?

In the vaſt, harmonious plan,

Inſect, fiſh, and beaſt, and man,

All adorn the gradual ſcale

From the ſeraph to the ſnail.

THE

VISION OF MOSES.

ON holy Sinai's solitary hill
Penfive the prophet sat, and much he mus'd
Of good and ill ; why pain, why sin, deforms
God's beauteous works: " What was th' Almighty's arm
" Exhausted by creating all those worlds
" That round us roll? was there no blessing left
" For this poor earth, this dungeon of distress,
" This vale of tears, this lazar-house of woe?
" Did we request thee, Maker, from the dust
" To force us into life? where virtue sinks
" Opprefs'd like the meek lamb, and vice uprears
" Its haughty branch, and spreads like flow'ring palm

" On Pison's banks.—O pardon, gracious Heav'n,
" My erring tongue; yet why should boundless pow'r
" So oft unjustly punish, and reward
" Astonish'd man?"—At this the mountain shook,
And groan'd thro' all her caves; a solemn voice
Like thunder heard remote, or rolling seas,
Swept by his trembling ear; " Rash child of man,
" Dost thou presume th' unfathomable depths
" Of my wise counsels to explore? arise
" Ascend this mountain's loftiest cliff, and thence
" Th' unbounded prospects view." With fault'ring steps
Fearing offence, the humbled seer obey'd.

He look'd, and saw wide territory spread
Before his wond'ring eyes; two bubbling brooks
Burst from beneath, and hurl'd their chrystal rills
Down to a grassy vale, that greedy suck'd
Th' enliv'ning moisture; there a fountain form'd

Besring'd

Befring'd with mofs, on whofe green banks appear'd
A loaded vine, whofe clufters ripe o'erhung
The fhaded waters, thither came anon,
Diftain'd with duft and gore, from fields of fight,
A weary warrior; from his panting fteed,
That champ'd a golden bit, alighting quick
On his red fpear he leant, and from his helm
The cooling chryftal quaff'd; to *Niger*'s banks
Gorg'd with fome pilgrim's blood, who rov'd forlorn,
O'er *Afric*'s fands, the lion thus repairs
To bathe his blood-ftain'd jaws; the chief refrefh'd
His fteed re-mounts, and fkims along the plain;
But of his lofs unconfcious, drops his gold,
Pearl, and Barbaric gems, the precious fpoils
Of a fack'd city. Piping o'er the plain
Next came a fportful boy, who eager fnatch'd
The chief's loft treafure, and with triumph ran
To meet his brothers, and with boaftful joy

The

The glitt'ring prize display'd.—Next soon appear'd
A wither'd, weak old man, trembling with age,
And bending to the grave, with staff in hand
To guide his tott'ring steps, and sat him down
To rest, attracted by the verdant scene.
The clust'ring grapes he cropp'd, and held to Heav'n
In humble praise, " Thou deck'st the florid earth,
" Parent of pleasure, maker kind, with herbs
" Nectareous, and ambrosial fruits, accept
" This rural sacrifice, ere yet I taste
" The juice divine !"—Then, after due repast,
His languid limbs by stealing sleep oppress'd
Sunk on the flow'ry couch: ere long he rests,
All burning with his loss, the chief returns
With hasty strides, and by the silver hairs
The trembling senior seizes, and demands
His casket stolen; with oaths, and tears, and vows
Of pleaded innocence the theft denied;

           To

To righteous Heav'n he calls, " With thunder cleave

" Thou mighty pow'r, who know'ſt our inmoſt ſouls,

" My lying tongue, if ought of treaſure loſt

" Theſe eyes beheld."—' Hence, hypocrite, to hell !'

With diſappointed rage the chief return'd,

' Old perjur'd villain, hence !' and plung'd his ſteel

With eager ſtabs thrice in his mangled breaſt :

Proſtrate the prophet fell, in mute amaze

Awe-ſtruck, yet wiſh'd t' expoſtulate, when thus

The voice divine preventing, him addreſs'd :

" Be ſtill, proud man, can thy all-piercing eye

" Thro' boundleſs ſyſtems darting view at once

" Connected worlds ? in a dim corner plac'd

" Of the vaſt theatre, from the ſcatter'd ſcenes

" The wond'rous plot unknown, dar'ſt thou revile

" The dramatiſt divine ? from broken ſounds

" Creation's univerſal harmony

" Preſume to judge ? whoſe inexpreſſive notes

" In

" In their full chorus reach not mortal ear?

" Could some pale glow-worm's ray who haply crawls

" Through the magnific pyramid, illume

" Those vasty vaults of darkness deep, and guide

" The gazing stranger through the sounding domes

" To *Cheop*'s chamber? reason's boasted lamp

" Is thus too weak to trace the mighty maze

" Of God's designs.—Ye little sons of earth

" In due proportion what can ye perceive

" Thro' the dim glass of gross mortality?

" Cease then to doubt, O son of man! nor blame

" The God of justice, Heav'ns all-seeing judge,

" Whose ways all mortal search elude; but know,

" Short-sighted as thou art, that base old man,

" Rolling in gore and shrieking now for aid,

" That infant's Sire, a midnight murd'rer! flew."

IN HORTO SCRIPT.

Auctore Thomâ Warton.

VOS O quæ fociis plicata ramis
Ulmi brachia panditis gemellæ,
Horti deliciæ, decufque parvi!
Dum vicina apium cohors per herbas
Fragrantes medio ftrepit fub æftu,
Fraternis tueamini magiftrum
Vos fub frondibus,, attici leporis
Auctores Latiive lectitantem;
Luftrantemve oculo licentiori
Colles oppofitos, aprica rura,
Laté undantibus obfitos ariftis,
Tectofve aeriis fuperne fagis.

The foregoing imitated.

I.

YE sister-elms, whose branches green
  In intermingling wreaths unite,
Of this my garden's humble scene
  At once the pride and the delight!

II.

As o'er yon fragrant plats the bees
  At sultry noon resounding stray,
In your dim arch reclin'd at ease
  Oh, shield me from the scorching ray.

III.

As all serene I turn the page,
  The chosen page of classic lore,
Of bards, whom warm'd with genuine rage,
  Or elder Rome or Athens bore.

IV.

Or as my roving eyes survey

    Yon sunny steep, my landscape's bound;

Its sides with waving harvests gay,

    Its top with airy beeches crown'd.

POLYDORE AND CLEONICE,

A TALE,

In Imitation of DRYDEN.

Non ita certandi cupidus, quam propter amorem
Quod te imitari aveo: quid enim contendat hirundo
Cycnis? aut quidnam tremulis facere artubus hædi
Confimile in curfu poffint, ac fortis equi vis.

His winding ftreams where ftrong Eurotas pours,
The fair Mifithra lifts her ftately tow'rs;
Mifithra fam'd of old for virtue's caufe,
For freeborn fpirits and impartial laws;
Tho' now fhe weep in chains tyrannic bound,
Her rage reprefs'd her glories in the ground.

Hither in arms from fair Italia came
Great Sigifmund intent on deeds of fame:
Of gen'rous troops he led a chofen train,
From Turky's fway the captive feat to gain.

Amid the croud diftinguifh'd from the reft
Two noble youths in birth and beauty bleft,
But for their mutual friendfhip more renown'd,
Shone in the lifts, and fought this hoftile ground;
Venice they left to warlike acts enflam'd,
This Polydore, and that Calliftus nam'd:
Early their fouls heroic deeds were taught,
Early their breafts the fire of friendfhip caught;
Beneath one banner fought the faithful pair,
And fide by fide, adminifter'd the war:
Thus match'd in arms, in high defcent the fame,
Affociates to the fields of Greece they came.

While thus Mifithra lay begirt with arms,
And felt the force of Sigifmund's alarms:
There dwelt within of race illuftrious born,
An eaftern maid, and beauteous as the morn:
Long many a Turkifh Lord had vainly ftrove
To gain the royal Cleonice's love;
Her charms had drawn from India's utmoft land,
Princes and Potentates of high command;
Oft their ambaffadors in full refort
Num'rous appear'd, and throng'd her father's court;
With richeft gifts th' unwilling maid to greet,
And pour'd Arabia's treafures at her feet.
But unallur'd by gifts, and grandeur's pride,
The gen'rous fair their dazzling fuit denied.
Not wealth or pow'r could win the virgin's breaft,
'Twas love alone could make her nuptials blefs'd.
The mercenary fouls whom gain invites,
In cold embraces meet, and uninfpir'd delights.

North

North of Mifithra's war-girt walls there ſtood,
Form'd of thick ſhade a venerable wood.
Where oft of old Sylvanus' ruſtic ſhrine,
Laconia's ſons ador'd with rites divine.
Remote and ſecret was the cloſe retreat,
And ſolitude had darken'd all the ſeat.
Nor had Italia's deep-embattled pow'rs
Extended their array beneath the ſacred bow'rs.

It chanc'd at noontide hour, one fatal day,
In breezes cool to calm the ſummer's ray,
The beauteous virgin to this ſecret ſhade,
Attended by her train of damſels ſtray'd:
There as regardleſs of impending fate
Beneath a branching pine the virgin ſat;
Sudden of coming footſteps ſounds remote,
Her liſt'ning ear with diſtant echo ſmote:

When strait a troop whom Polydore had sent
Detach'd on some design of deep intent,
On neighing steeds advanc'd in thick array,
And sought the gloom where Cleonice lay:
Alarm'd the virgin at the fearful sight,
Wing'd thro' the grove precipitate her flight.
But soon the rushing steeds outstripp'd her course,
That swift pursued her, with the lightning's force,
Soon caught an easy prey the panting maid,
That for her damsels cried, and shriek'd for aid.
Swift on their steeds the captive maid they bore,
And with their prize return'd to Polydore.
Soon to his tent with decent care convey'd
Regardful of her state the captive maid.

Beneath his tent brave Polydore they found,
Not with embattled troops begirt around,

But

But with the conſtant partner of his care,
He ſat retreated from the pomp of war.
His youthful prime his helm unbuckled ſhew'd,
While from beneath his auburn treſſes flow'd.
With graceful negligence a purple veil,
Floated redundant o'er his lucid mail.
A ſword emblaz'd with gems and Jaſper's pride,
Shone with conſpicuous luſtre at his ſide.
Thus ſat in converſe ſweet the faithful pair,
When enter'd at his tent the captive fair.
Graceful her look with grief and beauty mix'd,
And on the ground her ſtreaming eyes were fix'd.
Such lovely tears, and beauty thus diſtreſs'd,
To mild compaſſion mov'd his gen'rous breaſt.
And as he look'd, he felt the ſudden dart
Of love infix'd in his unguarded heart.
When thus, impatient of the kindling flame,
Th' heroic youth beſpoke the weeping dame:

" Fair maid, whoe'er thou art, whose heav'nly charms

" Have thus inflam'd my breast with love's alarms,

" Whom the sun's beam has ting'd with riper dye,

" Than boast the dames of northern Italy,

" Restrain, fair maid, your grief and streaming tears,

" Let dawning hope dispel those fancied fears:

" Once more Misithra's lofty town to greet,

" Safe I resign thee to thy native seat."

The gen'rous speech her grateful bosom fir'd,

Her eyes his arms and graceful youth admir'd.

His youth and graceful mein and rich attire

To touch her breast with mutual love conspire.

With secret fire the glowing virgin burn'd,

And this address with new-born hope return'd:

" O matchless warrior, whose unconquer'd might

" So oft has turn'd our bravest troops to flight,

" Nor

" Nor lefs in arms and warlike deeds you fhine,

" Than in a bounteous foul and virtues more divine.

" How can I e'er repay th' heroic deed

" A captive from the bands of flav'ry freed?

" Yet fince you thus ordain to fet me free,

" One fmall requeft I make with fuppliant knee,

" That thefe brave troops which me their captive bore,

" May fafe conduct me to my native fhore;

" Laden with precious gifts they fhall return,

" That high emblaz'd my father's courts adorn;

" Treafures that grac'd our anceftors of old

" Bracelets and ftarry gems and maffy gold,

" Spoils won from conquer'd provinces renown'd:

" With thefe rewards thy bounty fhall be crown'd."

Thus as fhe fpoke, her ardent eyes confefs'd

The mutual flame that kindled in her breaft.

When Polydore, who faw his love repaid,

In tend'reſt accents thus beſpoke the maid:

" Unbrib'd by gifts this ſquadron I command

" Safe to conduct thee to thy native land.

" Yet Oh what diff'rent paſſions rend my breaſt!

" Love grants, yet inly grieves at thy requeſt.

" And muſt we then thus part unequall'd fair?

" Muſt glowing love thus yield to cold deſpair?

" Can mutual paſſion point out no retreat

" Sacred to love alone and converſe ſweet?

" Deep-waving woods encloſe Miſithra's tow'rs,

" Nor has the ſtorm of war profan'd their ſacred bow'rs."

He ſpoke, with modeſt glance the nymph approv'd

His ſpeech, and ſilent ſhew'd how much ſhe lov'd:

Her through the camp at Polydore's command

To fair Miſithra leads a choſen band.

Meantime while Polydore his love expres'd
An equal ardor feiz'd Calliftus' breaft.
With earneft eyes her charms the youth furvey'd,
Though friendfhip's warning voice he ftill obey'd;
And impotent of paffion vainly tried
The ftruggling pangs of confcious love to hide.

Thus long the lucklefs youth in fecret pin'd,
While love and friendfhip diverfe tore his mind;
Meantime obfervant of the ftated hour
The happier lovers met within the fecret bow'r.
At length the haplefs youth, who knew the place
Sacred to love and Polydore's embrace,
Deeply revolving in his throbbing heart
How beft to heal his forrow's madding fmart,
Sought at the wonted hour the fatal fhade,
Refolv'd (O dire defign!) to flay the maid:

And

And tho' his foul abhorr'd the cruel deed
That the dear idol of his heart fhould bleed,
Yet this he thought the fureft way to end
His grief, and keep uninjur'd yet his friend.
Beneath a bufhy fhade conceal'd he ftood;
That when the maid appear'd within the wood,
With his bar'd fteel he might her breaft invade,
Ere Polydore could bring his timely aid.

How madding paffion and his black defign
With direful thoughts to fhake his foul combine!
He ftarted oft at each low-whifp'ring wind,
And thought he vengeance heard and Polydore behind;
And at each ruftling heard amid the gloom
Thinks 'tis th' expected Cleonice come.
In vain.—And now the murder he defign'd
Rifes in all its horror to his mind.

Each

Each moment adds a sting his conscious breast
To wound, and long delay reflexion dire encreas'd:
His soul could bear no more—when from his thigh
The deadly steel he draws resolv'd to die.
Within his breast he plung'd the shining blade;
When strait his hand uncertain and afraid
Stopp'd in mid-way by sudden doubt witheld,
Reason forbad; and quick its desp'rate force repell'd.
Forth from his breast his half-bath'd steel again
He drew, when fainting with the lively pain,
And in the tortures of his recent wound,
Of footsteps thro' the grove he heard the sound:
When starting at the noise, down dropp'd the blade
From his flack hand, and to the neighb'ring glade
With stagg'ring steps and faint alarm'd he fled,
From mortal view to shroud his guilty head.

'Twas

'Twas Cleonice's ftep that ftruck his ear,

Who duteous fought her wonted lover there.

The maid approach'd where in the path was laid

Dropp'd from Calliftus' hand the fhining blade.

She ftarted fudden as the fteel fhe view'd

In reeking drops of recent gore imbru'd.

But Oh what horrors in her bofom rofe,

Her ftiffen'd form what icy terror froze,

How ftood the virgin fix'd in dumb furprife

When on the ftudded hilt fhe caft her eyes!

The well-known-ftudded hilt whofe ftarry pride

She mark'd on Polydore bright-glitt'ring at his fide,

That fatal day when to the tent fhe came,

And kindled in his breaft the mutual flame.

She thought *his* blood had ting'd the blade with red,

And the befprinkled fteel befpoke its wearer dead.

But ah what dire miftake her mind poffefs'd

What falfe furmife involv'd her tortur'd breaft!

It

It chanc'd the fword that late her eyes admir'd

When Polydore with love her bofom fir'd,

Haply by Polydore that fatal morn,

Was for his own in friendfhip's freedom worn.

She fees in thought her bleeding lover lie,

And marks each gufhing wound with fancy's eye.

'Twas rage too mad for vulgar figns to fhow,

And folemn filence beft exprefs'd her woe.

She fnatch'd the fword that with the crimfon glow'd

(So thought the virgin) of her lover's blood,

And cried, when words the lab'ring paffion found,

" Let the fame point on both inflict the wound;

" 'Tis juft, fo faithful, and fo fond a pair,

" From the fame fteel the ftroke of death fhould fhare;

" Tho' thou, dear Polydore, art gone before

" I clofe purfue thee to the deftin'd fhore!"

She fpoke, and all on wildeft fury bent

Her mantle from her heaving bofom rent.

To

To the bar'd chest the deadly steel applied,
And in fresh streams of reeking purple dy'd.
Sudden each charm her with'ring cheek forsook,
And death's pale hue distain'd her dying look.
She fell and sinking, o'er her mangled breast
With decent care compos'd her blood-stain'd vest.

Scarce was she fall'n, advancing thro' the grove
When Polydore approach'd to seek his wonted love.
But ah what dire surprise what fears destroy
Th' imaginary scenes of fancied joy.
What horrors dash'd his dreams of wish'd delight,
When first the bleeding virgin met his sight!
In eager anguish o'er the prostrate dead
The grief-distracted lover bow'd his head.
On her cold lip a trembling kiss impress'd,
And with his hand explor'd her bleeding breast;

But

But the pale lip in icy death was froze,

And deadly cold her bleeding boſom roſe.

Then thus before the breathleſs maid reclin'd

He pour'd the ſorrows of his madding mind:

" What cruel hand has thus thy boſom gor'd

" What force againſt thy charms could lift the ſword?

" Where ſhall I find th' inflicter of the wound?

" Lo all is deſert ſolitude around.

" Ye foreſts conſcious of the ſavage deed

" Ye trees that ſaw my Cleonice bleed,

" Utter your voice, to my rack'd thought relate

" This hidden maze, this myſtery of fate:

" O why prevented not my ſpeed the hour

" That gave thee to the murd'rers ruthleſs pow'r?

" His unrelenting hand I might have ſtay'd

" Or ſhar'd thy fate in death beſide thee laid.

" But ſince to ſtop his vengeance was denied

" Or fall a willing victim by thy ſide;

" It

"It is not now forbade me to receive
"That death the ruthlefs murd'rer could not give."

He fpoke; and difengag'd with eager hand
The fword that yet in her faint grafp remain'd;
But ah no fooner fhone its hilt to view
Than trembling his Calliftus' fword he knew.
Then what mix'd paffions with united rage
And rebel tumult in his mind engage!
While thee, too faithful friend, in thought deceiv'd
The murderer of the virgin he believ'd:
At once the injur'd friend and widow'd lover griev'd.
Friendfhip prov'd falfe, difdain of life encreas'd,
And now with rage redoubled glow'd his breaft.
As Polydore with wild defpair enflam'd
The weapon at his naked bofom aim'd,
Ere yet he dealt the death-inflicting ftroke,
That inftant from the brake Calliftus broke:

By friendship call'd he left the shrouding shade
Where latent long the fainting youth had laid.
With duteous haste advanc'd he to prevent
His lifted arm, and stop the dire intent.
But Polydore ere yet he struck the blow,
When his thick-flashing eyes beheld the fancied foe,
With newborn rage and kindling fury burn'd,
And weak despair to fellest vengeance turn'd.
With lifted arm he met the wretched youth,
Nor stay'd to prove his faith or virtuous truth.
Deep in his breast he plung'd the well-aim'd blade
With eager rage, and as he struck he said,
" Hence to the darksome house of night descend,
" And feel the due rewards that faithless deeds attend.
" Be Zacon's bitter tree thy baleful food
" Far from the chaste recesses of the good.
" Hence to the shades, there seek some desert cell,
" Where only fiends, and shapes of horror dwell."

He spoke: the good Calliſtus ſunk in death
And pour'd in ſtreams of blood his ruſhing breath.

Now wretched Polydore alone was left
Alike of miſtreſs, and of friend bereft.
Pale, motionleſs, in deep amaze he ſtood
And view'd in dumb deſpair, the ſcene of blood.
'Till from his grief, theſe words a paſſage broke,
And thus in bitt'reſt agony he ſpoke:
" What foul deſign thy force, Calliſtus, mov'd
" To lift the ſteel againſt my beſt belov'd?
" Could neither beauty, love, or faith diſarm
" On bloody deeds intent thy murd'rous arm?
" Hadſt thou not ſullied friendſhip's ſacred name
" With this dire act, and ſtain'd thy better fame;
" Happy companions from a life well-ſpent
" To thoſe immortal regions we had went,

" Met after death, and in th' ambrofial groves

" An undivided pair renew'd our loves.

" Now forms terrific from that bleffed coaft

" Drive far away thy blood-polluted ghoft,

" That reftlefs wand'ring o'er the facred ground

" Would taint the purer air and breathe pollution round.

" Yet there my Cleonice fhall I find:

" With duteous hafte I follow faft behind;

" There blifs our yet imperfect loves fhall crown

" And all our woes immortal pleafures drown.

" But whither roves my grief-diftemper'd mind

" For prefent pangs a future eafe to find?

" Are thefe the triumphs, this th' expected fame

" For which in arms to Syria's feats I came?

" Are thefe the deeds of blood, are thefe th' alarms

" That Sigifmund expected from my arms?

" Who

" Who now perhaps stands loit'ring at my stay
" His ardent legions form'd in thick array
" And with impatience chides my long delay.
" To other scenes than those of glorious fight
" This fatal sword will aid my destin'd flight."
He spoke, and urging with impetuous force
The well-aim'd blade, sunk low beside the virgin's corse.
Oh luckless pair accept this pitying lay
Which to your shades with duteous grief I pay.
O early lost! to whose untimely tombs
Each due returning night fair friendship comes,
In grief reclining o'er your mournful urns,
Her vot'ries struck by fate so dire she mourns.
Nor thou disdain these rites fair Syrian maid,
Which here I offer to thy pensive shade.
Permit my muse to pay this grateful verse,
And hung with humble wreaths adorn thy hearse.

ALFRE-

ALFREDUS.

ISIS ubi lambit fœcundo flumine lucos
Pieridum fortunatos, dilectaque Phœbo
Atria, et extructas finuoso in margine turres;
Hîc deserta olim, nulloque nitentia cultu,
Prata, udosque agros, limosa obduxit arundo:
Vixque inter steriles juncos, ulvamque palustrem,
Lentis obscuræ serpebant flexibus undæ.

Hùc fortè *Alfredus* gressum tulit, arvaque circùm
Miratus, glebam irriguam et viridantia Tempe,
Tempe quæ sylvæ cingunt superimpendentes,
Hîc, inquit, profugæ secreto in littore musæ
Optatam inveniant sedem, gratoque fruantur

Hospitio, et tacitâ securæ in valle quiescant;

Nec locus ullus erit quo se plus jactet Apollo.

Pascua continuò micuere per avia turres:

Ipsa Isis vitreis nitidum caput extulit undis,

Suspiciensque novas arces, insuetaque templa,

Venturos lætâ præsumit mente triumphos,

Culminaque artificem *Wrenni* referentia dextram.

Nec tamen infausto posuisti has omine sedes,

Sancte Pater, nec spes animum frustrata fefellit;

Cernis, ut attollunt vivaces vertice lauros

Egregii Vates, et Phœbo digna locuti,

Quique omnes Sophiæ norunt decerpere flores.

Ipse agmen, cunctis sublimior, ordine longo

Chaucerus ducit; prisco dum pectine cantat

Cristatas turmas, equitesque hastilibus aptos,

Sive levis pangit fabellas ritè facetas,

Angliacumque aperit felici carmine Pindum.

Quis procul ille* autem, folus qui in valle reducta,

Lentior incedit, defigens lumina terræ?

Hic animæ latebras princeps patefecit opertas,

Unde illa innumeros motus, ratione magiftrâ,

Induat, unde ortu dubio primùm infita menti

Cognitio explicuit vires, tenebrifque refufis

Clara per obfcurum prætendit lumina callem.

Hunc olim Rhedycina canet, quotiefque recenfet

Grata fuos, celebrefque memor per fæcula cives,

Infignem ante alios felix memorabit alumnum.

Nec te, Caftalidum proles † lectiffima, plectro

Mufa ingrata filet, cui fontes ipfa reclufit

Integros Pallas, facilifque indulfit Apollo,

Mufæoque dedit contingere dicta lepore.

At neque dilectis folùm penetralia mufis

Condidit *Alfredus*, foli fua limina Phœbo;

* Locke. † Addifon.

Jura etiam fapiens et fervantiffimus æqui
Edocuit, quâque eft ftabilis Res Publica normâ:
Quin Artes, fautore illo, fubiere repentè
Ignotæ; tum Nauta vagus dare vela patenti
Aufus erat pelago, atque alienas quærere terras;
Contemnenfque æquor tumidum victricia claffis
Arma tulit latè, *Danis* dominata fugatis,
Et patrium advexit peregrina in regna Draconem.
Quinetiam Artifices externâ e gente profecti
Illius accitu coeunt; pars mænibus urbes
Cingere, folertique manu fuperaddere formas
Spirantes, vivofque excudunt marmore vultus;
Dum calamo intereà varioque colore figuras
Mentitur veras, et ludit arundine Pictor.
Nec minùs in bello Virtus infigniit hofti
Parcentem victo, debellantemque ferocem:
Nam neque ventofo tulit hunc in prælia curru
Ambitio, neque Regnandi tam dira cupido
         Impulit

Impulit infando vicina laceſſere regna
Marte; ſed infidi cum fædus rumpere *Dani*
Auderent, nutu novit componere bellum,
Et conjuratis potuit dare jura Tyrannis.

O quis me ducet quà *Farringdonia* clivo
Aſſurgit viridi, ſublimi a vertice montis
Lætus ubi intentos paſcens per ſingula viſus
Explorare humiles campos, ſubjectaque poſſim
Mœnia, et eductas non nullo numine turres;
Hîc ulmos inter patulas caput erigit alma
Alfredi nutrix *Wantagia*, ſæpe ſub umbrâ
Hâc puer, agreſti meditatus arundine Muſam;
Sæpe hanc ad lympham, ſubductæ in margine ripæ,
Parvulus incerto ſe luſu exercuit Heros.
Colle ex adverſo candenti e rupe minacem
Surgere equum,* rudibuſque notis expreſſa videbis

* White-horſe hill.

Tendere

Tendere terga folo, longoque albefcere tractu.
Hìc olim ftravit duro certamine *Danos*
Alfredus, poftquam defeffa Britannia longo
Servitio, imperiumque pati plagafque fuperbi
Victoris nollet, rurfùfque repofceret arma.
Hinc procul apparet felix Rhedycina, remotis
Indiciis, mediâ riguæ convallis in umbrâ;
Vixque acie poffunt oculi fervare domorum
Tecta, et cœruleis occultas nubibus ædes;
Has inter veneranda, immanique arduâ mole,
Radclivii ftat pulchra domus, medioque fuperbit
Ampla fitu, qualis *Vaticani* inclyta fedes
Erigitur cœlo, aut Capitoli immobile faxum
Subjectam latè profpexit defuper urbem.
At propè moliri cernas nova culmina,* eodem
Radclivio fundante, viden', jam Turris aperto
Emicat afpectu, propriumque affectat Olympum.

* The Obfervatory.

Et

Et mox tempus erit, cum certâ lege Planetas

Errantes, magni attentos ad juſſa Parentis,

Newtoni explorent alii, qui fædera noſcant

Naturæ, arcanaſque vias, ut menſtrua luna

Accendit ſub noĉte facem, radiiſque relucet

Oppoſitis, medio dum Sol immotus in axe

Igne indefeſſo fulget, cinĉtuſque miniſtris

Ipſe regit ſeriem, et volventes ordinat annos.

Muſarum auguſtæ Sedes, ſacrataque teĉta

Quæ cœlo æquavit pietas, et opima priorum

Munera condecorant, Salvete, ut perculit ardor

Cor mihi, dum recolo priſci monumenta Laboris,

Et decus antiquum, et tantæ primordia famæ.

Tuque O Sanĉta Domus,* longâque ætate Verenda,

Cujus in hoſpitium, quâ primum ſede receptæ,

Alfredo monſtrante, choros duxere Camænæ,

* Univerſity College.

Ante alias, Salve! celebrat dum mufa Patronum

Communem, veterique refert hæc Vota Parenti;

Intereà tu firma diu, longofque per annos

Stes immota, novo furgentes vertice turres

Confpiciens, fociofque Lares circùm undique cultu

Magnifico, qualis patrii per limen Olympi

Invehitur Regina Deûm, turritaque tollit

Tempora, et innumeros complectitur Una Nepotes.

ANTIPATRI EX ANTHOLOGIA.

QUÆ natas peperi novem beata
Viginti et pueros, nec has vel illos
Abreptos gemui repentè letho.
Haud natos etenim meos Apollo
Telis abftulit, aut Diana luctu
Puellas graviore profequendas.
At contrà hæc minuit meis dolores
Partûs adveniens, et advocatus
Apollo pueros virile ad ævum
Morborum variâ cohorte tutos
Provexit, viden' ut frequente prole
Et linguâ, Niobi antefto, modeftâ.

INCERTI

INCERTI AUCTORIS EX ANTHOLOGIA.

TELLUS alma senem hunc sinu foveto
Recordata gravis tibi laboris.
Stirpem semper enim premens olivæ
Ornavit, Bromiique vite multâ;
Inducensque satis aquas sequaces
Implevit cerere, et colendo fecit
Omnis plenam oleris, feramque sylvam
Novâ arte Alcinoi vigere pomis.
Ob quæ terra levis tegas capillos
Canos, et vario lepore florum
Distinguas tumuli virentis herbam.

CALLIMACHI EX ANTHOLOGIA.

TRISTES, O Menalippe, manè inani
Corpus condidimus tuum fepulchro:
Quin mentis foror impotens eâdem
Occifa eft Bafilo die, fuapte
Manu, fcilicèt haud tulit fuperftes
Fratri vivere quem pyrâ cremârat.
At verò ob duplicem anxiumque luctum
Ariftippe pater tibi univerfa
Cyrene doluit, videns vigentem
Olim prole domum orbitate mœftam.

INSCRIPTIO.

Hinc exit qui mox arentia prata rigabit
Atque cavatâ hortos in margine lambet olentes
Amnis, abundanti fœcundans pafcua fluctu:
Nilo par Ægyptiaco, licèt ille facratos
Fontes Æthiopum penitùs fub montibus abdat
Aut ipfo jactet ftirpem deducere Olympo.

UXORI

UXORI OPT.

Hos tibi mittit malè tuta flores
Ripa, mi conjux, neque tu colorem
Simplicem fpernas, quòd hyems negârit
    Veris odorem.
Sed magìs ferves hyemale pignus
Veris, et finu foveas amato
Quæ tibi gratus referat benignæ
    Dona maritus.

ELEGIA.

MISTA dolore ægram pertentant gaudia mentem,
  Vixque erumpentes contineo lacrymas;
Ut turres Ventæ oppofito de colle viator
  Defpicio, et patriæ culmina nota domûs:
Luminibus madidis occurrit plurima imago,
  Quæ quondam juveni gaudia vera tulit.
Atria per deferta aulæ regalis hirundo
  Pennâ iterat folvi non metuente fugam.
Saxa inter disjecta vetuftæ in margine foffæ
  Frigentes auras captat anhelus equus:
Hunc circumvolitant indefeffo agmine mufcæ,
  Dum glebas putres ungula crebra ferit.
Vifa procul per prata udis interlita rivis,
  Multa recèns tonfo vellere balat ovis;

Dum

Dum madida exficcans grex vellera fole tepenti
Lentis afcendit paffibus alta jugi;
Quà latè oftendit vallum Catharina vetuftum,
Danorum, et fylvâ tectum apicem viridi.
Beauforti juxtà turres renovataque templa,
Adverfo illimis fole relucet aqua.
Quà creta albefcens ripam diftinguit utramque,
Ægrè difficili cymba movetur equo.
Jamque augufta fonat fani campana vetufti,
Wiccamicâque exit lenior arce fonus.
Nec mora, pullatum portis effunditur agmen,
Affuetoque frequens murmure fervet ager.
Ludite felices, dum perbrevis hora juventæ,
Jucundique oti tempora grata finunt.
Ludite, nec vobis, medio de fonte lepôrum
Gaudia quod lædat furgat amari aliquid.
Ah! ne, quæ vatem huc ufque eft comitata mifellum,
Curarum vobis ingruat atra cohors.

ARCHIÆ EX ANTHOLOGIA.

NATUS præcipiti tener Lyſippes

Accedens ſcopulo, eſt periclitatus

Tuum, O Aſtyanax miſelle, fatum :

At mater revocavit alma, mammam

Nudam pectore proferens, ſimul quæ

Et letho puerum fameque ſolvit.

PARMENIONIS EX ANTHOLOGIA.

TENUIS læna mihi fat eſt modeſto,
Nec flores Heliconios per hortos
Depaſtus, dapibus potentûm opimis
Hoſpes ſerviam, opes mihi peroſæ
Faſtûs ſtultitiæque quæ parentes.
Haud fingam ſatrapi cüique vultum:
Libertas humilis dapis mihi ſit.

DIOSCORIDIS EX ANTHOLOGIA.

ME vernam tumulo tuum reponis
Magis qui dominum deceret ipfum
Quod curæ puer es mihi, Timanthes.
Sit felix, fcelere et foluta, vita.
Sin me adveneris ob gravem feneĉtam,
Tuus fim Domine orco et in nigranti.

ANTIPATRI EX ANTHOLOGIA.

AGNUM lanigerum unicamque vaccam
Solas Tityre opes cafae tenebas:
Ifti egere foras famem moleftam.
Ambos perdere fors tibi immerenti.
Agnus dente lupi, dolore partûs
Nitens difficili juvenca lapfa eft.
Sic grex deperiit cafae tenellus.
Quin et vir miferande tu reflexo
Collo de trabe mortis aufus atrae
Nodum nectere, per domum vacantem
Jaces, ampliùs haud ovis fonantem
Suetâ voce, bovifve mugientis.

INSCRIBED ON A BEAUTIFUL GROTTO NEAR THE WATER.

BY THE REV. T. WARTON.

THE Graces fought in yonder ftream,
  To cool the fervid day,
When Love's malicious Godhead came,
  And ftole their robes away.
Proud of the theft, the little God
  Their robes bade Stella wear;
While they, afham'd to ftir abroad
  Remain all naked here.

IDEM

IDEM LATINE REDDITUM.

VICINIS nuper Charites dum nuda fub undis
  Geſtibant medio membra levare die,
Advolitans, temerè quas ripæ in margine veſtes
  Depofuere Deæ, furripiebat *Amor*:
Quas puer exultans furto, lætufque rapinæ,
  Purpureas Stellæ donat habere meæ.
At Charites pavidæ fugere, et veſtibus orbæ,
  Atque hoc delituit fingula nuda fpecu.

EX ANTHOLOGIA.

Hic, precor, in prato viridanti membra, viator
    Paulifper, longo feffa labore, leva.
Hìc Zephyro quaffæ captabis murmura pinûs,
    Hìc tibi dulce melos multa cicada canet:
Vicinifque jugis te demulcebit avenâ
    Paftor, fub platani tegmine, propter aquas.
Hìc medios vitato æftus; cras, I pede faufto,
    Hæc memorans, " fueram Pan, tuus hofpes, heri."

AN ARS SIT PERFECTIOR NATURA? AFFIRMATUR.

COLLE sub exeso Belindæ dædala dextra
    Divinâ patulam condidit arte domum:
Non hìc coralium splendet de fornice rubrum,
    Non pandit varias lucida concha vices;
Non pario surgunt exsculpta sedilia saxo,
    Nec fons artifices itque reditque vias:
At viridem muscum per saxa humentia rore,
    Serpentesque hederas callida Virgo dedit.
Quà libet abrupto de pumice desilit unda,
    Rarus et incultam pingit acanthus humum.
Haud ultrà veneres jactet natura, puellæ
    Cum valet artificis dextra referre pares.

AN LOCUS CONVENIAT LOCATO?
AFFIRMATUR.

PRÆRUPTÆ rupis gelido sub vertice, Martis
    Sublimi assurgit culmine magna domus:
Hinc exaudiri ventorum verbera sæva,
    Qui portæ circum stridula claustra fremunt;
Porta adversa ingens solidoque adamante columnæ
    Quas ferri cingunt robora, Martis opus.
Intùs sanguineo *Rabies* accincta flagello,
    Dentibus et crepitans pallidus ora *Timor*:
Illìc est, vitæ curas lucemque perosum,
    Morti immaturæ quem sua dextra dedit;
Nant oculi, rictuque patent foeda ora rigenti,
    Horrida stat putri sanguine cæsaries.

Illic fubridens irato *Infania* vultu,

Et membra occultans fparfa cruore *Phonos*.

Tali Threicius gaudet focio agmine Mavors,

Talis et armorum convenit aula Deo.

AN CASUS ET FORTUNA SINT IN REBUS? AFFIRMATUR.

D RYDENUS suavi musarum instinctus amore
  Avia Parnassi per juga tendit iter.
Jamque *Sigismundæ* infelicis funus acerbum,
  Crudelisque refert improba jussa Patris:
Jam super *Æmiliâ* missas in prælia turmas,
  Ruptaque amicitiæ fœdera prisca canit:
Cymonemque docet molli mansuescere flammâ,
  Quam lentè insinuans *Iphigenia* ciet.
Dein *Cleopatræ* audet pollenti pectore fortem
  Edere, & in tragicos fortior ire modos.
Detractâ, mox ingressus penetralia Phœbi
  Virgilii lauro, tempora cingit ovans.

Pierio quanquàm confperferit omnia melle,

Tinxerit æterno cuncta lepore licèt;

Vix Lar Drydeno certus, propriique Penates,

Et quod fama affert, fors inimica negat.

INCERTI AUCTORIS EX ANTHOLOGIA.

Nostri fit lapis hic, Sabine, parvus
Amoris monumentum, amice, largi:
Te quæram affiduè; domoque Ditis
Mei ritè memor, modò hoc datum fit,
Ne Lethæi aliquid bibas liquoris.

——DULCIQUE ANIMOS NOVITATE TENEBAT.

Cum primum indocili pulfaret pollice chordas,
 Informifque lyræ barbara fila Jubal;
Turba coit fratrum, infuetæ miracula vocis,
 Atque novos circum ftat venerata fonos,
Credula, quod tales poterat fudiffe loquelas,
 Tale melos, conchæ numen ineffe cavæ.
Non etenim argutæ nemorum per opaca volucres,
 Non querula e prono quæ cadit unda jugo,
Mulfiffent unquam fimili dulcedine mentes,
 Quæve per umbrofas perftrepit aura domos.
Scilicèt obftupuit turba hæc indoéta rudifque
 Vocis inauditæ capta canore novo,
Quam mufæa mele chordæque juvare nequiffent,
 Quas digito Organici mobiliore cient.

IN SYLVA SCRIPT.

CUR plaufis trepidè, palumbe, pennis
Me nulli generis tui nocentem
Fugis, dum pede pervagor licenti
Secretas nemoris vias opaci.
Tuæ vocis enim fub arbore iftâ
Murmur flebilitèr gementis olim
Angorem nimium levare fuevit.
Talis nempè querela, quanquam iifdem
Modis fit repetita, pectus ægrum
Æquè commovet, ac melos süave
Quod fundit Philomela vere primo.

PICTORI EGREGIO THOMÆ BEACH.

O Tu qui calamo nimis fideli
Veros exprimis indolis colores
Et vultûs fimul, hanc levem camænam
Manfuetè accipe, quæ licentiori
Modó, folvere vult tibi benigno
Grates, vix lepidas fatis parefve
Manûs egregio tuæ labori.
Ah ne te fpecies inanis unquam
Famæ, quæ fugitiva ludit ufque
Viros qui vitreum colunt honorem,
Subducat proprio ftylo tenacem
Adhuc ingenui et meri lepôris.

Tuum est, sitque diu, rudis popelli
Laudes spernere, nec tibi timor sit
Quin et posteritas beata sano
Tandem judicio, tibi rependat
Veros, quos meruisse laus, honores:
Et ritè annumerabit inter Artis
Primos, *Parrhasios* vetustioris,
Knellerosque recentioris ævi.

EPITAPHIUM ANNÆ STAINES.

ERGO te Pietatis, Anna Mater,
Exemplar fideique terra condit
Heu luctu graviore profequendam!
Te morum facilem, ingenîque lenis,
Nepotes recolunt tui frequentèr.
Te blandamque operam tuam requirit
Frater, jam fenio gemens inerti,,
Quæ fic fedulitate mollicellâ
Senectæ folita es levare curas,
Et miti poteras tuâ loquelâ
Dies fallere jam moleftiores.
At te longa quies premit jacentem,
Quæ ferò aut citiùs manebit omnes.

FINIS.

www.ingramcontent.com/pod-product-compliance
Lightning Source LLC
Chambersburg PA
CBHW030245170426
43202CB00009B/637